BARBED WIRE UNIVERSITY

BARBED WIRE UNIVERSITY

*The Untold Story of the Interned
Jewish Intellectuals Who Turned an Island
Prison into the Most Remarkable School in the World*

DAVE HANNIGAN

Guilford, Connecticu

An imprint of Globe Pequot, the trade division of
The Rowman & Littlefield Publishing Group, Inc.
4501 Forbes Blvd., Ste. 200
Lanham, MD 20706
www.rowman.com

Distributed by NATIONAL BOOK NETWORK

British Library Cataloguing in Publication Information available

Library of Congress Cataloging-in-Publication Data

Names: Hannigan, Dave, author.
Title: Barbed Wire University : the untold story of the interned Jewish
  intellectuals who turned an island prison into the most remarkable
  school in the world / Dave Hannigan.
Other titles: Untold story of the interned Jewish intellectuals who turned
  an island prison into the most remarkable school in the world
Description: Guilford, Connecticut : Lyons Press, [2021] | Includes
  bibliographical references and index.
Identifiers: LCCN 2021036028 (print) | LCCN 2021036029 (ebook) | ISBN
  9781493057702 (cloth) | ISBN 9781493063529 (epub)
Subjects: LCSH: Hutchinson Internment Camp (Douglas, Isle of Man)—History.
  | Jewish refugees—Great Britain. | World War, 1939-1945—Concentration
  camps—Isle of Man. | Aliens—Isle of Man—History—20th century. |
  World War, 1939-1945—Great Britain. | World War, 1939-1945—Evacuation
  of civilians—Great Britain. | Isle of Man—History—20th century.
Classification: LCC D801.G7 H36 2021 (print) | LCC D801.G7 (ebook) | DDC
  940.53/174279—dc23
LC record available at https://lccn.loc.gov/2021036028
LC ebook record available at https://lccn.loc.gov/2021036029

♾™ The paper used in this publication meets the minimum requirements of American National
Standard for Information Sciences—Permanence of Paper for Printed Library Materials, ANSI/
NISO Z39.48-1992.

To my sister Denise

Contents

ACKNOWLEDGMENTS

It started with a podcast. Stuck in traffic on the Long Island Expressway, I happened upon a conversation between Dan Snow and David Baddiel on History Hit about the internment of Jewish refugees on the Isle of Man during World War II. Not something that ever cropped up in the classrooms of my youth in Ireland, I was intrigued by the story, especially when I discovered the way in which the internees of Hutchinson Camp had created an ad hoc university and entertained themselves with art, plays, and classical music. This book is the result of my subsequent obsession with the topic.

As per hoary old cliché, there are too many people to thank, but it would be remiss of me not to express my immense gratitude to Niels Aaboe for his enthusiasm, encouragement, and support in the early stages, and to Rick Rinehart for coaxing the project over the finish line. Elsewhere at Lyons Press, Lynn Zelem did a wonderful job nursing the book through production, and Melissa Hayes, bringing her exceptional editing skills to bear, made some serious improvements to the manuscript. The quality of the fantastic layout by Wanda Ditch is evident in your hands today.

During an illuminating week in Douglas, Isle of Man, the redoubtable Yvonne Cresswell and her colleagues at Manx National Heritage were enormously generous and ridiculously obliging. Similarly, the staffs of the Tate Archive and the Imperial War Museums in London and the Leo Baeck Institute in New York.

Daniel Mirecki was kind enough to talk about his father Adolf and to sketch the curious journey he made from Ukraine to the English Midlands. Equally generous, Peter and David Furth shared photographs and a magical VHS video they had made of their father, Hans, recounting his truly remarkable life story. Patrick Mooney, curator of a fantastic website on Hermann Fechenbach, was a tremendous help with photographs and other details about his tale.

Debts of various kinds are owed to many, many people. A by no means conclusive list includes PJ Browne, Dave Clarke, Tommy Conlon, Paul Howard, Fergal Keane, Deirdre McCarthy, Enda McEvoy, Michael Moynihan, Colm O'Callaghan, Rob O'Driscoll, Kadie Pearse, Bill Raniolo, Ger Siggins, and Denis Walsh.

More than three decades have passed since I first walked into University College Cork (Ireland) as a freshman and started to hang around with Gavin O'Connor, Emmet Barry, Mark O'Loughlin, Fergus Roche, Ken Cotter, and Mark Penney. Fresh-faced boys then, definitely middle-aged men now, yet true friendship has endured in the most wonderful way through the years and across the oceans. An honor to know ye all.

For continued professional support I would like to thank Malachy Logan and the sports department of the *Irish Times*.

For nearly two decades, I have found a home very far from home at Suffolk County Community College in Selden, New York. My colleagues in social sciences there—especially Al Cofone, Denise Haggerty, Judy Travers, Michael Benhar, and Mary Kaffaga—have given me friendship and so much more. Particular thanks on this occasion also to Jill Santiago and Jodi Moran at the campus Center for Social Justice and Human Understanding, featuring the Holocaust Collection, for their invaluable assistance with various aspects of the project.

I am eternally grateful to my brother Tom, sister Denise, and niece Kadie, and their respective families, for everything, and they are always in my thoughts even as the pandemic has kept an ocean between us for far too long. I would also like to give special thanks to George and Clare Frost for their continued support, and to their daughter Cathy for giving me three wonderful sons.

Abe, Charlie, and Finn remain the lights of my life and are so incredibly tolerant about long ago losing the dining room table to an ogre lurking behind an unruly mountain of books and papers who tells them to shush way, way too much.

Any mistakes are, of course, my own.

—Dave Hannigan, April 2021
East Setauket, New York

PROLOGUE

THE OLD MAN HELD THE WOOD PANEL IN HIS HANDS, EYED THE engraving of a nude woman, and smiled at the art dealer. Now, he knew why he'd been called here. He ran his fingers along the edges, inspecting the familiar grain, and recalled instantly what it was and where it came from. A swatch of mahogany, it once belonged to a piano that was played by the more musically gifted residents with whom he once shared an internment camp. Until the day it was deemed broken beyond repair, and then the artistic inmates set about plundering it to glean whatever materials they might be able to deploy in their work.

That was 1940. Now, nearly half a century later, in his mid-seventies, Klaus Hinrichsen stood in a showroom in London, smiling at the memory of how some of the most gifted German and Austrian sculptors and painters of their generation were reduced to cannibalizing a defunct instrument. Deprived of proper resources, men like Kurt Schwitters, Siegfried Charoux, Fred Uhlman, and Fritz Kraemer regarded nearly every found object as a challenge to their ingenuity and an opportunity to showcase their talent. They once even asked Hinrichsen if they could cut his impossibly long eyebrows so they might harvest the hair for their improvised paintbrushes. The desperate lot of the artists imprisoned behind barbed wire.

Even if there was no signature on the wood, this etching wasn't the work of any of those artists, however. That much Hinrichsen knew. The moment he traced the outline of the portrait of a lady that seemed to be Salome performing the dance of the seven veils, he recognized the handiwork. The depth of the cut gave it away. This was unmistakably a piece by Ernst Müller-Blensdorf, carved with his unique style, during that part of World War II when the British government deemed them all enemy aliens, to be placed under armed guard on an island in the Irish Sea. The authorities called their new home on the Isle of Man "Hutchinson Internment Camp." History would come to know it, with good reason, as "the artists' camp," or the "Barbed Wire University."

CHAPTER ONE

Guests of the Nation

This accusation I make and make in the plainest terms. In this country, as in France before reaction threw aside all pretense, a deliberate and systematic intimidation of liberal-minded foreigners is going on. So that even while we are actually at war with the Axis Powers and their subjugated "allies," people in positions of authority and advantage in this country are allowing the collection, internment and ill-treatment of all those disaffected subjects of our enemies who would be most willing and able to organize internal resistance in their own countries on our behalf.
—H. G. WELLS, "J'ACCUSE," *REYNOLD'S NEWS*, JULY 28, 1940

THE MARATHON TRAIN JOURNEY THAT BEGAN AT KEMPTON PARK ended at Liverpool docks. The men disembarked there and started marching again, two by two. As they did, some of the locals who had gathered to witness the curious spectacle of the new arrivals started to shout abuse and to spit at them. Like they were the actual bad guys. Like they were, really, truly, fifth columnists hiding out in plain sight as part of some great Nazi conspiracy. Not a gaggle of mostly Jewish refugees who had spent much of the previous few years trying by every means possible to resist the inexorable rise of Adolf Hitler and then struggling to escape his perverted wrath.

Gobs of spittle flew toward Klaus Hinrichsen and his companions as they shuffled along, tired, disoriented, and more than a little nervous, pathetic figures toting small suitcases in their hands. Finally, the hulking HMS *Tynwald* came into view at dockside and they realized this was the next leg on their odyssey.

Weeks earlier, what was ordinarily a passenger steamer operating between Liverpool and Douglas on the Isle of Man had seen sterling service as one of the ships pressed into emergency assignment, saving British soldiers fleeing the Nazi press at Dunkirk. With a capacity of nearly two thousand, no other vessel had delivered more men to safety during the mission. Now, the hero of that hour was, effectively, a prison transport vessel for men who had also fled the Nazis. How else to describe it as armed guards ushered these startled-looking passengers across the gangway?

The boat was a babel of languages. Whispered conversations in Yiddish. Angry declarations in German. Dramatic arm-waving in Italian. They passed the journey talking of what they had already experienced, the horrors of the different transit camps. Hinrichsen soon discovered that his stay at Kempton Park, for all its problems, had been top-class compared to the deprivations of Warth Mills, near Bury, where two thousand internees had been kept in a building containing eighteen taps and one bathtub. Things were so bad there that the Red Cross eventually forced its closure.

As had become part of the ritual, there were murmurs on board about exactly where they might be headed. Nobody in authority would tell them, so the more fanciful speculation centered on Australia and Canada, both of which were known to be destinations for deportees during the war. Hinrichsen was smart enough to know that this particular vessel wasn't capable of a journey of that magnitude. Still, the lack of knowledge or awareness (most of these men knew little of the geography of the British Isles) meant that a wave of fear swept through the ship when after five hours or so, landfall beckoned.

Initially, the men were shocked, then scared. From a distance, the port where they were obviously going to land had flags waving that when they fluttered in the coastal breeze looked suspiciously like swastikas. On closer inspection, the symbol thankfully wasn't that. It was the triskelion, the three-legged motif of the Isle of Man, a British territory eighty miles from Liverpool, halfway across the Irish Sea to Dublin. Most of them had never heard of the place before. Now, it was somewhere they would never forget as the ship cruised past the Tower of Refuge, built a century earlier to provide safe haven for sailors who had run aground in Douglas Harbor.

Once the *Tynwald* docked, names were called and the men were separated into groups. Hinrichsen had been assigned to Hutchinson Camp. While those destined for other locations waited for their transport to arrive, he and his cohorts were ordered to start walking again. Their journey took them along a once-scenic waterfront now necklaced with barbed wire and battle stations, as if preparing for an imminent invasion. The resort where so many Britons had come to enjoy happy holidays during previous decades had been transformed into a military dystopia, Victorian hotels and guesthouses with their sea views interrupted by a vista of armed soldiers with bayonets drawn, marching their charges between the rolling lengths of barbed wire.

They didn't have far to walk through Douglas. The cortege strolled along the promenade and then turned left up the steep hill abutting the Villa Marina, ordinarily a destination for those in search of music, or even prayer when it hosted religious festivals. These bemused men were oblivious to the local landmarks as they straggled up the incline, still ignorant of exactly where they were heading, growing weary and hungry, most having eaten just a piece of bread and cheese over the previous twenty-four hours.

Hinrichsen had come to know some of his fellow prisoners in the course of their travels, but he was not yet aware that this nondescript bunch included so many gifted writers, artists, musicians, and professors. Trudging up those streets from the dock, nobody could have imagined that this forlorn group might create something so wonderful and enduring from their time in captivity in this strange land. And that Hinrichsen, as de facto cultural officer, would preside over so much of it. That was all in the near future.

At the top of Stanley Terrace, the convoy came to a sudden halt by the main gate of a place called Hutchinson Camp.

"The higher we walked, the more marvellous the view we got over the sea below," remembered Hinrichsen. "But then we entered through fantastic barbed-wire constructions. And there were spotlights, and we were greeted by a sergeant-major."

The Camp was made up of four streets, three of which consisted of bow-fronted Edwardian boardinghouses surrounding a rectangular patch of perfectly manicured lawn. An attractive and rather quaint setting in ordinary circumstances, much less so after it had been pockmarked with double rows of barbed-wire fencing, and gated off by armed guards. The absurdity of the situation was hammered home by the presence of a miniature golf course among the shrubbery—more evidence that here was a place where people traditionally came to have fun, to enjoy a break from real life.

Until now, when reality was intruding in the worst way.

Nearly one thousand men arrived in the first intake on July 13, 1940. There were just thirty-three houses. The math wasn't difficult to compute. Even allowing for the fact that these buildings were configured as bed-and-breakfasts to put up holiday-makers from the mainland during the island's high season each summer, this wasn't just going to be a tight squeeze; it was going to be seriously overcrowded.

"We weary and bedraggled travellers were scrutinized when we arrived late in the evening, with some distaste by an extremely smart Regimental Sergeant-Major, Mr. Potterton, who in civilian life had been head porter of the Dolphin Square blocks of flats in Chelsea," said Hinrichsen. "He counted out thirty to forty men, appointed one of them as leader, and allotted a house to each group."

With a gaggle of others, Hinrichsen walked along the street searching out No. 19 Hutchinson Square, his new home away from home. There, he would spend days and nights over the coming weeks and months asking the same questions. Why did the British government do this? Where was his family in Lübeck? How long was he going to be made to stay? Was it possible to get word to his girlfriend Gretel that he was okay? Did anybody care that they were even here, or were they destined to be stranded and forgotten?

And the toughest question of all: How had he ended up here?

The Gestapo came for the Hinrichsen men on Kristallnacht. As the remaining Jewish businesses and synagogues in Lübeck were being attacked and ransacked that November night in 1938, Felix Hinrichsen and his two eldest sons were manhandled onto a truck and taken in for questioning. For years, they had feared this night was coming, sensing in the deteriorating political atmosphere that something like this was increasingly inevitable. That was why the Jewish population in this corner of Schleswig-Holstein, which numbered more than six hundred in 1930, had shrunk so much it could by then be counted in double figures.

Most were originally Sephardic Jews who had arrived in Northern Germany around 1640, having previously fled the terrors of the Spanish Inquisition in Portugal a century before that. The Hinrichsens, a long-established family in the region, had once been bankers to the dukes of Mecklenburg. Felix had chosen a different path, becoming a partner in a respected law firm. Since Adolf Hitler had become chancellor in 1933, however, he had found work as a lawyer more and more difficult to come by, the latest batch of regulations restricting him because of his background to handling cases only for the dwindling population of Jewish clients.

The ironic thing is, Felix had actually renounced Judaism, converting to Christianity in his early twenties in order to marry his wife, Ida, the couple choosing to raise their kids in the Lutheran faith. If abandoning the religion of his birth wasn't enough to spare him from this persecution, it did ensure that his sons were eventually released by the Gestapo after Kristallnacht. The powers that be officially judged them to be "half-Aryan."

Klaus Hinrichsen was twenty-five years old the night the Nazis came to the door, a grown man whose fledgling career as a wannabe art historian had already been stymied by his Jewish lineage. A grown man who realized this latest reprieve from the authorities meant a call-up to the German army was an inevitable next step in the process. A grown man who decided to get out while he still could.

Having resolved to try to escape their clutches, he wrote to distant relatives in England desperately seeking an invitation to come visit London, to conduct art history research. While awaiting a reply, he threw himself into assisting the remaining Jewish families in the area seeking to emigrate. As a "half-Aryan" who knew a thing or two about how to evaluate art and antiques, he negotiated on their behalf with tax officials and government departments, as many sought desperately to buy or bribe their way out.

Finally, the letter inviting him to England arrived, enough collateral to persuade the army recruitment office to give him a three-month travel pass. He arrived in London in June of 1939, and, almost immediately, telegrammed his parents informing them that, in a terribly unfortunate accident, he'd broken his leg, a phantom injury that meant he would have to stay longer than planned. When they told the German authorities of his unlucky break, the Lübeck branch of the Red Cross sent him a care package of cookies in the shape of swastikas—a bizarre reminder of the deformed society he was fleeing.

Once in London, like many German and Austrian émigrés, Klaus Hinrichsen soon found himself visiting Woburn House, where the Quakers were doing their best to assist new arrivals, each of whom was gifted a booklet entitled "Helpful Information and Guidance for Every Refugee." It offered all manner of advice to the newcomers; among the eight commandments was one admonishing them not to criticize British mannerisms, and another reminding them to appear grateful to their host country.

Obviously identifying him as something of a renaissance man (at school he had edited a magazine dedicated to German romantic poets), the Quakers enlisted Hinrichsen to serve in their theater group, an acting troupe that turned up at the canteens of factories in London's grimy East End to provide lunchtime entertainment and relief from the drudgery to workers.

He picked up another job, too. In the mid-1930s, he had done some freelance work for *Thieme-Becker*, a specialist art publication, and that was enough to land him a gig representing the English interests of a Swiss publisher of international medical periodicals. With some philanthropy and a modicum of professional progress, this quite promising start to life in exile was bookmarked by a fortuitous meeting with Gretel Levy, a nineteen-year-old cook at Hampstead General Hospital, on September 2. She was seven years his junior, yet a young woman with a story not dissimilar to his own.

A native of Pomerania, Gretel told him she had come to London to learn English at the age of seventeen, and once she saw the dastardly direction Germany was headed, decided to stay. In the summer of 1938, her parents had beseeched her to return, trying to assure her that the worst Hitlerian excesses against the Jews were over, and that the country would soon come to its senses. Having initially found the coldness of England off-putting, she still reckoned it a safer long-term option than Nazi Germany. She refused to go home. Four months later, her father was killed in the rampages of Kristallnacht.

When she met Klaus Hinrichsen, Gretel was instantly smitten. He was handsome and attractive, but it was much more than that. He also reeked of education and had a bearing and a certain charm about him. Theirs was going to be a love story. Eventually, and after a fashion.

The young couple's fanciful romantic notions were immediately shattered the morning after their initial meeting when Prime Minister Neville Chamberlain announced the declaration of war on the radio. Everybody knew the day had been coming, but for the Germans in England's capital city, life changed immediately. For starters, most of them opted never to speak their native tongue in public again.

"Once the war broke out, I didn't speak German," said Levy. "Hardly at all. People couldn't understand why there were people walking around speaking German, even in Hampstead."

Some took other drastic action, too, changing their names. Gretel decided from that point on she should be called Margarete, as it was less obviously Germanic. A smart move, because in the initial weeks of war, there was a mild hysteria sweeping through Britain regarding the estimated seventy thousand Germans and Austrians in their midst. Although it was known that at least 80 percent of that number were Jewish refugees fleeing the increasing terrors back home, that fact didn't count for much in certain eyes.

"Many of these immigrants are Jews," wrote George Ward-Price in the *Daily Mail* in October 1939. "They should be careful not to arouse the same resentment here as they have stored up in so many countries. I dislike as much as anyone the Nazi persecution of that race, but it is fact that the Jews were getting a stranglehold on German life out of all proportion to their avowed numbers. Many of the German Jews, often themselves recent immigrants from Eastern Europe, were the worst of their kind. In this country, the national character is strong enough to absorb the better Hebraic type; in Germany, the Jewish aliens found a class-conscious, self-interested community and the misdeeds of some brought down reprisals on the rest."

This type of alarmist hate-mongering explains why Ward-Price had, over the previous years, earned a reputation as Hitler's favorite British journalist.

In the first few days of the conflict, the authorities quickly swept up just under five hundred Germans and Austrians, those who had been previously identified by MI5 as Nazi sympathizers and potential spies. In a matter of weeks, all foreigners over the age of sixteen were compelled to attend hastily arranged alien tribunals where they were sorted into different categories, from A (those deemed a high risk to national security, numbering just under six hundred) to B (those on whom some suspicion rested, numbering just around nine thousand) to C (sixty thousand or so, who were reckoned to be essentially loyal to Britain).

Established in October of 1939, these rather ad hoc courts were strange, mostly genteel affairs usually presided over by county court judges and members of the local bar. The Quakers and other refugee charities were often present to assist those being evaluated, as were members of the local constabulary. However, there were inevitable logistical problems given how many tribunals were being held across the country. Interpreters were not always on hand, so in one celebrated case a harmless German poet was deemed Category A—by virtue of the fact that he spoke no English—and he was instantly interned.

Some areas of London had to process hundreds of cases each day, and a few individuals ended up being wrongly classified just because of the indecent haste to get the job done and a concomitant desire to err on the side of caution. Hinrichsen had no such bad luck and could speak for himself in court. So, like most in his situation, he was correctly deemed to be Category C. Initially, this meant there were no restrictions placed on his movement and very little real impact on his life in exile.

Still, it's an indication of how the British government was thinking that as early as April of 1939, five months before war broke out, it had also put in place plans to house eighteen thousand foreigners if a more wide-scale internment was deemed necessary. And pretty soon, it was. Why? Well, the first phase of the war went badly for Britain and France, and this spawned a burgeoning paranoia about the possibility of a German landing somewhere on England's east coast. Fear and scaremongering about this threat was a constant in the right-wing press, and when the Netherlands fell, the screeching in the newspapers was amplified by Sir Neville Bland.

On May 15, Bland, Britain's representative at The Hague during the capitulation of the Netherlands, circulated a memo in government circles claiming the Dutch defeat had been made possible and greatly facilitated by a "fifth column" of Germans living among them. He ended his report with a call for all Germans and Austrians to be arrested and interned in order to preempt the same thing happening in England.

That call was echoed by author and playwright Beverley Nichols in a piece for the *Sunday Chronicle* which alleged every refugee was now a potential domestic terrorist.

"Why should we be blown up as we are walking over a bridge unless it is strictly necessary?" asked Nichols. "Or poisoned by contaminated water or hit on the head by the local gasworks as it descends to earth? No, sir. The letters readers send about Germans who are going free in their own district would make your hair stand on end."

Obviously, Nichols had never heard of the Quakers and of the vast majority of Germans like Hinrichsen who had assimilated quickly, and, in Hinrichsen's case, spent his spare time doing charity work to ameliorate the plight of London's working poor. Nuance was just another casualty of the war. By the middle of May 1940, however, even Category C aliens like Hinrichsen suddenly found themselves under increased scrutiny.

All citizens of Germany and Austria living on or near the coastline from Inverness in Scotland to Dorset in South West England, a vast territory deemed vulnerable to a German invasion, were taken into custody. Within days, the net was cast even wider. All male aliens between the ages of sixteen and sixty who had been Category B were to be arrested and interned. Up to this point, the only restrictions placed upon these individuals had been to forbid their ownership of cameras or bicycles.

The increased vigilance/paranoia was kind of inevitable. Aside from the daily diet of high-profile writers and journalists demanding that Downing Street take drastic action ("ACT! ACT! ACT! DO IT NOW!" screamed a *Daily Mail* headline calling for internment), the deteriorating military situation after Dunkirk and the arrival of Italy into the war on the side of the Nazis pushed newly installed Prime Minister Winston Churchill to take the ultimate step against the country's Italian community. "Collar the lot!" he famously declared at a cabinet meeting, discussing the necessity of securing the homeland.

That colloquial instruction evolved into an order to arrest and intern all Germans, Austrians, and Italians, regardless of their previous categorization, and was followed up with a lengthier public explanation of the tactic on June 4.

"I know there are a great many people affected by the orders which we have made who are the passionate enemies of Nazi Germany," said Churchill in the House of Commons. "I am very sorry for them, but we cannot, at the present time and under the present stress, draw all the distinctions which we should like to do. If parachute landings were attempted and fierce fighting attendant upon them followed, these unfortunate people would be far better out of the way, for their own sakes as well as for ours."

As one of these unfortunate people, Hinrichsen knew by then that his arrest was imminent. They would come for him like they were coming for everybody else like him. If "Collar the lot!" reeked of a certain urgency at the highest level of government, the actual rounding up of the foreigners was a lot more haphazard, bureaucratic, and less dynamic than Churchill's tone might have presumed. In most cases it fell to the local policemen to pick up the potential fifth columnists living in their precincts. Word quickly spread in the immigrant community that some of the bobbies on the beat weren't going out of their way to fulfill the task.

"If you left your house before seven in the morning and went into Hyde Park or the West End or anywhere and came back after five p.m., you couldn't be interned because whoever did the interning at the time, they had office hours," said Hinrichsen. "And if you did stay out, you couldn't be interned. And many people did. Apparently, there was a complete exodus from Hampstead down to Lyons Corner House [a restaurant] and back in the afternoon. But at that point I hadn't been long enough in England, and I thought [that] if they are going to intern everybody, they are going to intern everybody . . . [but] it was simply [that] they had a quota—they wanted so many every day."

In one case, a policeman got fed up with calling upon the same German target without any luck, so he resorted to leaving a note asking him to stay home the following day in order to be arrested. And, bizarrely, he did, and he was.

The circumstances of Hinrichsen's eventual internment were not dissimilar. By then, he was living in a tiny attic flat on Glenlock Road, near Haverstock Hill in Hampstead. Upon returning one evening, the lady who owned the house broke the news to him.

"They are coming for you in the morning," she said.

"Why?" he asked.

"Well, they came with the name of Walter Bergmann but they had arrested him already. So they said, 'Have you got anybody else?' I said, 'I have got Mr. Hinrichsen.'"

Twelve hours later, there was a knock on the door and Hinrichsen, a small suitcase with toiletries already packed, found himself under arrest and on his way to the local police station. From there, he was later put on a bus, driven across London, and out to the leafier suburbs of Surrey. Nobody told him where he was headed. Speculation among passengers was that their ultimate destination was the Isle of Man, because that's where Britain had interned Germans during World War I. For some, it eventually was. For now, this leg of the journey ended at Kempton Park Racecourse.

Ordinarily a venue full of whooping and hollering racegoers enjoying a day out, celebrating or lamenting gambles on the horses, it had been transformed into something completely different. Through the bus windows, Hinrichsen saw large army tents pitched on the Central Lawn, an area that had been ringed with barbed wire. These were the sleeping quarters of 1,500 Grenadier Guards, the security detail on duty at the racecourse.

Many of them had just returned from active service on the front in France, and their attitude toward the men they were guarding varied greatly. Some were sympathetic—especially once they realized a lot of these individuals had just risked their lives and spent fortunes trying to escape from the grip of the Nazis, only to find themselves imprisoned in England. Others regarded them as enemy combatants and treated Hinrichsen and all the others accordingly.

A few of these soldiers strolled up and down with drawn pistols in their hands as if a shoot-out or attack was imminent, pointing bayonets at anybody they felt was stepping out of line—a threatening sight that frightened many of the internees. The older men, some of them veterans of World War I, scoffed at these attempts to intimidate them. As part of the new arrivals' induction, the commanding officer gave a speech to the internees in which he confessed to being severely disappointed that he wasn't in charge of a camp full of *real* prisoners of war, denouncing these hordes in civilian clothes as mere "rabbits."

Every square inch of the racecourse was needed to house the growing population. The vast majority ended up sleeping on straw mattresses beneath the grandstand where, at night, they gave thanks that in England the summer of 1940 turned out to be much hotter than normal. The quality of the toilets depended on where in the grounds you were billeted. The very, very lucky ones were placed in the Royal Enclosure and got to use bathrooms there that were, literally, fit for a king. Their less fortunate peers—just about everybody else, including Hinrichsen—soon found themselves squatting in holes in the ground when the Kempton Park toilets proved unable to cope with the sudden influx of 1,500 semipermanent residents.

The plumbing problems were indicative of how ill-conceived the whole operation seemed to be. In the opening days, there was a lack of sufficient food as the supply lines struggled to get up to speed with the demand for providing three squares a day to those being held. There were security issues, too. Some internees, afforded more time by their arresting officers, had arrived at Kempton Park with valuables, including cash, typewriters, and books—items that they later alleged were pilfered by errant soldiers from the Grenadier Guards.

As per a normal prison camp, everything was rigidly timed, and there were two roll calls each day. Lunch was served at 1:00 p.m., supper at 7:30 p.m., and lights-out was at 10:30 p.m. Inevitably, cliques formed. Orthodox Jews huddled together. Communists, too. Most internees just loitered, wondering what strange fate the British might have in store for them. Others gossiped and speculated about the identity of fellow inmates. Celebrities in their midst included Captain Franz von Rintelen, a legendary German spy during World War I; Prince Frederick, a great-grandson of the Kaiser himself; and a Nazi official who was reportedly a former adviser to Joachim von Ribbentrop, Hitler's foreign minister.

Trying to figure out who was a friend (escaping Hitler) or foe (working for him) was a way to pass the time for Hinrichsen and others during the first days of their captivity in the Kempton transit camp, especially since nobody told them where they might be headed, or when. They knew only that this was a temporary billet. Everything else was speculation.

Hinrichsen finally got his answer on the morning of July 12, 1940, when he was told to pack up before being marched toward a nearby train station.

To fortify them on the seventeen-hour train journey north from Kempton Park to Liverpool, Hinrichsen and his fellow travelers were handed a portion of bread. Then, a large block of hard cheese was apportioned to be divided up between everybody in the carriage—a difficult task to achieve without cutlery on hand. Some men reached into their suitcases for razor blades before remembering that all sharp objects had already been confiscated.

Finally, a solution to the problem was at hand. A bizarre solution that summed up the strangeness of the entire situation. The internees asked the soldiers guarding them for assistance, and they thought nothing of breaking off the bayonets from their rifles and handing them to the prisoners. Then they watched them slice away and distribute slivers of cheese from seat to seat. It was indeed a curious relationship between the guards and those they were guarding, when one handed a sharp and deadly weapon to the other and then watched them put it to work before politely handing it back.

"We had young soldiers guarding us," said Hinrichsen. "And one of those young soldiers played around with his rifle. Took it to pieces and couldn't get the thing going again. So, we had to help him."

If the sight of a guard asking his prisoners to assist him in reassembling his weapon summed up the absurdity of the situation these men found themselves in, the odd nature of their predicament hit home again on arrival at Hutchinson Square. As they filed through the gate, the soldiers barked out orders in the tone of men running an internment camp, even as the physical layout of the place made a mockery of that status.

"We were very pleasantly surprised there were houses and they had furniture," said Hinrichsen. "The great amazement was when we turned on the lights [and found] there were no curtains. [When] we turned on the lights, the light bulbs were red and the windows were painted blue."

The mystery of this curious color scheme would soon unravel itself.

CHAPTER TWO

Windows on the World

A wide view, the blue sea, eternal freedom lies ahead of us. Where are
we? On the top of these houses that is our temporary refuge just now.
And when we climb down and go outside all we can see is our limited
world which somehow appears unreal to us but which all the same can
teach us a lot sometimes.
　　　　　　　　　—GUSTAV HIRSCHFIELD, HUTCHINSON CAMP,
　　　　　　　　　　　　　　　　　　　　NOVEMBER 24, 1940

THE LUFTWAFFE BEGAN BOMBING THE CITY OF LIVERPOOL ON AUGUST
9, 1940. For fifty nights over the next three months, German planes
rained terror down on the people below, a sustained and forensic campaign designed to destroy the largest port on England's west coast, a
location crucial to the British war effort. From their new home eighty
miles to the northwest on the Isle of Man, the inmates of Hutchinson
Camp could often make out the distant glow of the fires lighting up the
sky to their south. On a clear day they saw sinister plumes of dark smoke
billowing into the clouds from the fiery ruins of the ongoing Blitz.

　　With Liverpool the second most-targeted city in Britain after London, the residents of the Isle of Man also had to be prepared in case their
island was specifically targeted. It wasn't. The only bombs that dropped
there were by mistake. But, each night, the internees heard the chill-
ing thrum of German bombers passing overhead, flying through their
airspace on the way to deliver deadly cargo to Belfast farther off to the

northwest. With so much potent air traffic in and around the area, the Home Office in London issued strict instructions about how the various camps should prepare for the possibility of air raids.

In lieu of blackout curtains, every window in Hutchinson Square was to be painted completely blue. Why? Because the houses were also going to be fitted exclusively with red lightbulbs. Aside from giving every kitchen the bizarre air of a boudoir at the best of times, some pen-pusher in the Home Office asserted that the blue paint would negate the red light.

Commander Hubert Owen Daniel was the man charged with implementing this policy and explaining it to the rather bemused internees, some of whom believed the curious paint job had been his personal idea. Having fought in France in 1915, winning a medal and rising to the rank of captain in the 9th King's Liverpool Regiment, Daniel had reenlisted at the outbreak of World War II and been assigned to oversee what would become Hutchinson Camp. In between the two conflicts, he'd built a career as an advertising executive with Unilever in London.

As camp commander—or commandant, as some referred to him—he gained a reputation for fairness, dealing with the men with a degree of humanity at all times. There were whispers he drank too much and, inevitably, complaints that he stuck too rigidly to the rules handed down to him from on high. Despite carping from a few that he didn't quite appreciate the circumstances of the situation with his optimistic refrain about being "a happy family," Daniel did improve living conditions and tried to be egalitarian in his dealings with men from all strata of society.

"In this camp," he declared, "the Oxford professor will not be treated any better than the scavenger among you."

At times, he appeared driven by a bizarre competitive desire to make Hutchinson the "best" of all the camps on the island, as if such a thing could—or should—be measured. Whatever his motivation, he did work to enhance their lives with schemes that ranged from building showers to adding beer to the menu to doing everything possible to allow classes to be taught and art to be made. Camp leaders who spoke to him on a regular basis vouched that he did listen to their criticism even if, often hidebound by army bureaucracy, he was not always able to take action regarding every critique.

Some later griped, with justification, that he proved flexible enough when affording unique privileges to a few higher-profile residents based on their reputation in music or painting or literature beyond the barbed wire. Those instances of rule-bending stand in contrast to another incident where he sentenced an overly romantic internee to three days in prison after he was caught throwing flowers through the fence to his fiancée. Arguments about inconsistencies in his policies would come much later. Around the square, it was Daniel's job to ensure that the painted windows did their job when the air raid sirens wailed. And that was sometimes easier said than done.

One of the residences was reserved for Orthodox Jews, and rules in the so-called "Kosher House" were obviously different than everywhere else around the square. Which was fine most of the time. Except when one air raid came on the Jewish Sabbath. When the sirens sounded, every light in the camp went out immediately, except at the Kosher House. No observant Jew could touch the switch on the holiest day.

"Put the f**king light out!" screamed Commander Daniel into the public address system that could be heard all over the camp. To no avail. A messenger was dispatched at great speed to inform the more devout residents of the need for instant darkness. The possibility of bombs landing might have been considered real and pressing, but for these internees, their religious laws took precedence.

"Are you a Jew?" the Orthodox men asked the messenger.

"Yes," he replied.

"Then, you cannot touch the light. To do so would be a sin," they informed him.

The messenger sprinted back to the commander's hut, where Daniel was now growing apoplectic with rage. A search began for a Gentile who could turn off the lights in the Kosher House. It says much for the demographics that none could be found in a hurry. Eventually, one man who said he was half-Jewish was unearthed and sent to do the needful. By the time the light was safely put out, the sirens had stopped wailing, the danger had passed, and Daniel's blood pressure began to subside.

That comic interlude aside, the painted windows were to prove a cultural boon for the men of Hutchinson. Well, after a fashion. Initially, they were regarded as a curse, a force of darkness that removed the only natural light from the houses—one more depressing feature adding to the air of unreality and the problem of timelessness besetting a group of men whose lives had been turned inside out and upside down in the space of a few weeks. Eventually, something had to give. And it did, when one of them couldn't take it anymore.

"One day an extremely hot-tempered artist named Hellmuth Weissenborn could not stand the blue-painted windows any longer," wrote Klaus Hinrichsen. "With the help of a razor blade, he started scratching off the irritating blue at the front window of No. 28 with the intention to clear the window and to let in the bright light of the summer evening. Nothing else. Perhaps somebody had already done the same in other houses, mechanically, stubborn. Weissenborn, however, at once recognized the graphical possibilities to develop new technique by carving [a] big space out of the blue, thus lighting the room behind the windows. In the fields which he spared came to shape fabulous creatures."

In his rage, Weissenborn had created a new art form of sorts. In a way, this was exactly the type of thing his life up to that point—his roundabout journey to this camp on the Isle of Man—had prepared him to do.

Born in the eastern German city of Leipzig on December 29, 1898, his father Fritz was an artist and a teacher, so Hellmuth Weissenborn grew up in an environment where creativity was fostered. "When I was six years old, and maybe even before, to draw or to model was our daily life," he said. "There was not a day as a child when I didn't model or make some drawings."

That idyllic childhood came to an end when Weissenborn was called up to fight for his country in World War I, at the age of just sixteen. The teenager saw action as a machine gunner with the infantry in Estonia, Russia, and at the Battle of Arras in 1917. As the conflict waned in the autumn of 1918, he was redeployed to the border between Macedonia and Serbia. He only found out the war was over after his regiment had crossed the Danube into Hungary on barges in December, a full month after Armistice had been declared.

Upon returning home, he gained a PhD in anthropology from the local university while simultaneously studying art at Leipzig Akademie. He eventually became a professor there, relishing the chance to work in an institution that prided itself on being at the cutting edge of graphic art, cherishing a job that allowed him to embark on his own career fashioning bookplates and designing books. His personal life was flourishing, too. He met and fell in love with Edith Halberstam, daughter of a well-known family steeped in the city's lucrative fur trade.

"A Weissenborn family photo album shows the pleasure-filled life that Hellmuth and Edith led: motoring in the countryside to the lakes to sunbathe and swim, laughing in cafes, riding motorbikes, relaxing with a group of friends," wrote Anna Nyborg in her biography of Weissenborn.

The romantic portrait of a couple of swells enjoying a full life in the Weimar Republic disguised the fact that the Halberstams were not thrilled about the relationship. Firstly, Hellmuth was not Jewish, and secondly, although he was a serious academic and artist, this placed him significantly farther down the social ladder than their daughter. When the couple married on April 21, 1931, Edith was immediately cut off from her family.

And there were darker clouds looming on the horizon.

"I was at a fair at the Augustusplatz in Leipzig the day I heard the Nazis had taken power," said Weissenborn. "Suddenly, their flags were hoisted in the square and everybody lifted their arms to give the salute. I refused, until my Jewish wife informed me it might be the only way to get out of the place without any trouble."

Soon, the Nazis, conscious of controlling all aspects of culture, imposed a Nazi Party member on the Leipzig Akademie as deputy director. Then, Weissenborn had an argument with the maid at his house. This dispute prompted her to go to the authorities to report subversive comments she'd heard him make at home about the Führer and the new regime.

"And that was a lot of stuff," he later confessed.

The Gestapo interviewed his colleagues and Akademie staff, and the clock was suddenly ticking on his tenure. A notice of dismissal finally came, citing that, like Socrates, the way Weissenborn was teaching a class on "Perspective" was somehow dangerous to the city's youth. He knew that there was much more involved in this allegation than some spurious academic critique of his work.

"By now National Socialism had run wild," wrote Weissenborn. "My son Florian was then about six; now he was destined to grow up as a second-class citizen, so my intention to seek a new existence in exile became a certainty."

Right before departure for England, where Edith had good connections, Weissenborn was informed that, as a World War I veteran, he could still save himself. If he apologized for what he had done, he might receive a pardon and be reinstated as a professor. This was in late 1938. But Weissenborn had no desire to remain in a nation increasingly enthralled by the Nazis, a place so rancid that Weissenborn's father—a man who'd volunteered to fight in World War I, at age forty—became a socialist to show his opposition to the fascist regime. Time was of the essence, too, because Hellmuth was still of eligible age for the military himself, and he feared getting called up to serve Hitler.

Even though London was the epicenter of the British publishing industry and Hellmuth brought references from highly rated German institutions and artists, work wasn't as easy to find as he'd hoped. Some of his new design concepts were regarded as avant-garde by the English houses. Still, he settled into his life in Notting Hill Gate, the assimilation made significantly easier by the fact that Edith retained a private income even though estranged from her parents.

Determined to earn his own living, he started a wood-engraving business out of their flat. Soon after that, he received the call to appear before the tribunals set up by the British government to establish whether aliens from the Axis Powers should be considered friends or foes. Unlike so many other Germans and Austrians who found themselves suddenly in the dock, Weissenborn spoke decent English and had a character witness in an old friend, the writer Victor Bonham-Carter, who testified that Hellmuth was "a friendly alien."

His official classification was Category C, one of those deemed to be no threat at all. At least, until Churchill issued the order to "Collar the lot!" That directive came in May of 1940, and by then, Weissenborn's marriage was also in trouble. He was living apart from Edith and Florian when two policemen knocked on the door and told him to pack a suitcase for his transportation to Warth Mills, the disused cotton mill in Bury, outside Manchester, the most Dickensian of all the temporary internment camps.

Like everybody who spent any time there, Weissenborn despised the place. Aside from the horrific living conditions and the shortage of food, there was the uncertainty. He couldn't stand not knowing where he was going next. Was he going to be shipped abroad? Was he going to stay here in this dreadful institution for years? To pass the time, he resorted, of course, to art, producing a linocut print that showed the camp yard, encircled in high barbed wire, with the chimneys of neighboring mills belching smoke in the background. When Major Baybrook, commandant of the camp, was shown the piece, he demanded an apology from the German.

After the gloom of his short-lived stint at Warth Mills, Weissenborn knew the moment he arrived on the Isle of Man that Hutchinson Camp, with its almost genteel rows of houses, was something completely different. Something much better. Sure, there was overcrowding, but that paled in comparison to his previous abode, where fighting among residents and stealing by guards had been common occurrences. In Douglas, he had arrived somewhere much more palatable for a man of an artistic bent.

Even before discovering that the general population included Kurt Schwitters, Fred Uhlman, and so many other artists, Weissenborn found a new home, in the kitchen of No. 28.

In every house in Hutchinson a call went up on the first day, looking for volunteers to cook. Most eschewed the task for fear that surely nothing decent could be rustled up from the available rations. Weissenborn answered the call, for no other reason than he figured it would be a way to pass the time and to stop him thinking about the terrible uncertainty of his situation. In his quest to keep himself occupied, he happened upon something of a vocation.

"I remember the first day we got herrings, Manx herrings," said Weissenborn. "It was fantastic! I grilled them. And, suddenly, with that, the whole atmosphere changed. All the men were saying, 'Oh Weissenborn, these herrings, they taste like trout!' And from then on I was, of course, favored in the house. I not only cook[ed] the lunchtime or the breakfast but also the evening meal, which was usually rather meager. I cooked some broth, celery or vegetables, made every evening a big soup so everybody was really satisfied. That helped my position enormously."

Weissenborn soon gained a reputation as the finest cook in the entire camp, an accolade earned, in part, by his happy knack for maximizing the resources available. That required getting everybody to realize the sum could be greater than the individual parts. Once the men were allowed to receive food parcels from relatives, some hoarded the ingredients they received and let them go to waste rather than share. At least until Weissenborn persuaded those in his house that pooling their raw materials would improve the variety and quality of meals for all on a more regular basis. He even introduced a rule banning his fellow internees from taking bread to their rooms.

One day, the cook from a neighboring house was in the kitchen when he asked Weissenborn what smelled so good. He opened the oven to reveal a roasting chicken, the bird having been stolen by another resident when he was sent out of the camp to work on a nearby farm.

If his culinary skills won him admirers, Weissenborn also needed the work to take his mind off his own problems. Edith had sent divorce papers to the camp, and now the two letters he and every resident were allowed to write per week had to be used to write to lawyers as he sought to extricate himself from the marriage. He also battled constant concern about how long this sentence might last.

"If I would have known at the beginning that I would have been interned for six months or a year, I would have taken it with humor," he said. "Not knowing was devastating. It wasn't so much the treatment, which was quite fair and human[e], but the fact alone to be imprisoned was, to me, something which is beyond my endurance. Fighting is less horrifying than being in prison. The worst was that I expected that we would be there for the duration of the war, and if Hitler would come over to this country and be victorious we would be handed over to him. That prospect to me was like a concentration camp."

A man with a lot on his mind, then, Weissenborn eventually took umbrage at the blue paint defacing the windows, and set about doing something about it.

"It looked like we were all underwater," he said. "We couldn't see. I immediately took a razor blade and started to scrape some out, and I made a few figures from classical mythology. That was quite interesting."

Interesting and groundbreaking. In a camp full of artists often frustrated by the lack of materials available, Weissenborn had created new art, literally, from scratch. More than that, he had fashioned something beautiful from a blue paint canvas that had previously served as a constant reminder of their oppression.

In his first attempt, he carved the goddess Artemis on a hunt. Soon, he added a unicorn, a figure riding a dolphin, a centaur, and the quintessentially English image of St. George fighting the dragon. In the kitchen, he etched out images of favorite meals that added greatly to the atmosphere, further improving the mood of his fellow residents.

Others quickly cottoned on to the artistic possibilities afforded by the dreadful window paint. Ernst Müller-Blensdorf went to work on the front window of No. 19 and the top floor of No. 37. A sculptor who, in the early 1930s, had taught at the prestigious Staatliche Kunstschule at Wutterpule near Düsseldorf, Müller-Blensdorf etched nude scenes that were erotically charged, especially for a group of men cut off from their wives and girlfriends—and all female contact—from the moment they were arrested.

One showed a naked couple sitting together in contemplation; another captured a man using magical powers to make the waters of a spring spray over the two women in his company. These images were enough to get No. 19 dubbed "The House of the Bathing Girls." For a group of men who worried about rumors the British had put bromide in the porridge to suppress their sexual urges, Müller-Blensdorf's creations were almost pornographic in nature.

Hinrichsen preferred to see them in a more elevated light. "As in his sculptures," he wrote, "Müller-Blensdorf combined in these windows a touch of gothic spirit with the formal strength of his own style, thus reviving ancient elements by means of modern artistic expression."

Others were equally ambitious. In No. 9, Anton Lowenthal, a young textile designer from Vienna, caused some controversy among house-mates and around the camp when he etched a rather ugly-looking man, beneath the caption, "What a pity Eve took that apple!" To provoke fur-ther debate, he had carved Adam and Eve on the windows on either side of the older gentleman, each of them carrying an apple with the price tag 1½ d (about 1½ pence in pre-decimal currency).

Everywhere the new artistic craze caught on as individuals, armed with nails, penknives, or razor blades, set to work converting the drabbest part of their prison into something beautiful. At once an act of expression and defiance, they stood in the windows and let their imaginations run free.

Mr. Lowry decided the men of No. 17 might benefit from viewing windows freshly decorated with lobsters, cigars, whiskey, and other ren-derings of the finer things they may once have enjoyed in the lives from which they had been so abruptly removed. Somebody else in the building carved a queen of hearts in homage to one of his housemates who was a notorious cardsharp.

In No. 5, Mr. H. Halpern attempted to rework parts of the Sistine Chapel in Rome, a curious addition in a camp that was predominantly Jewish. Indeed, the Orthodox Jews were so taken with the quality of Weissenborn's original work that they asked him to re-create images from the Old Testament on the windows of the Kosher House.

"I made a lion and other scenes, and they were very grateful to me," he said.

The internees, who sometimes walked the length of the camp just to peruse the windows into various worlds, had no shortage of animals to marvel at. The residence at No. 40 was known to all as the "Zoo House" because of the tableau its windows presented to the residents. While the quality of the engraving was a little less polished and more technically primitive, the sheer quantity of images on show caused many men to stop, stare, and marvel at the array of wild creatures etched meticulously into the paint.

The man behind these scenes was Hans Brick, aka Johann Neunzer. That he went by two names hints at the richness and complexity of his biography. Even by the standards of this diverse group of inmates, Brick's was a life story beyond compare. His father was mauled to death by a tiger he was performing with at the Nouama Hava Menagerie in Italy in 1889. His mother, originally Dutch, was so shocked by the news that she went into premature labor, and eventually died giving birth to Hans on November 4 of that year, in Nuremberg, Germany.

The tragic circumstances and the location of his arrival into the world (the German birthplace in particular) dictated much of what happened to the child thereafter. Initially cared for by Heindrick and Babette Neunzer, friends of his mother, he was christened Johann Georg Neunzer. For reasons unknown, his guardianship eventually fell to a man called Adler, an old colleague of his father's from the circus trade. Once he was deemed old enough, Johann went on the road and, following in his father's footsteps, became an animal wrangler. Although, in reality, he was much more than that.

With Circus Strassberger, Circus Blumenfeld, and Circus Busch, Hans Brick—as the billing introduced him in the big tops—traversed the globe, even touring Egypt and China. Along the way, he did a little bit of everything, working as a clown and performing high-wire and trapeze acts. His extraordinary ability with animals, however, marked him out from his peers, and it was in this role he began work at Chessington Zoo, twelve miles outside London, in its opening season in 1933.

Photographs from that period show Brick placing his head completely in the mouth of Rosie the Elephant, an animal that eventually became problematic in his absence because she only responded to the German's commands. Similarly, there are images of him cavorting with Habibi, a full-size lion with which he developed what some in the company believed was a telepathic relationship. At a time when animal acts were big enough box office draws to be featured on Wheaties boxes in America, Brick gained a reputation as a daring crowd-pleaser.

The public came to see him climb fearlessly into the cage with the wildest of creatures and then playact with them. One minute massaging Habibi's legs as if preparing him for a prize fight, all the while gurning for the audience, the next lying beneath a Bengal tiger and toying with him like a child manhandling a favorite teddy bear. In 1930s Britain,

Brick became a boldface name in the circus and zoo industry. Of course, his celebrity counted for naught once the war broke out and every German-born resident, no matter their tenuous relationship with the country, was deemed suspect.

In his first few weeks at Hutchinson, Brick shared his extraordinary story with his fellow internees. No doubt some considered his yarns to be tall tales. How could they not? This sharp-faced, perpetually grinning character claimed to have once trained a traveling troupe that included a rhino, a macaw, a parrot, a hippopotamus, two goats, a chimp, a zebra, and a giraffe. Eventually, his credibility was established and, pipe usually perched in his mouth, he gave formal talks as part of the camp's ongoing education program, entertaining everybody with accounts of gamboling around the jungles of Africa, trapping various creatures in the wild.

Although part of his boasting included the fact that he never used whips or sticks to get the animals to do his bidding, one of his party tricks around Hutchinson Square involved using a homemade whip to lasso the heads clean off of flowers from twenty feet away. Some days he deployed the same weapon to catch scurrying mice. No small feat. That dexterity was nothing compared to the story he told of teaching Habibi to fire a dart from a spring gun, to go fetch it, and then to return and drop it at Brick's feet. Even more stunning than this coup de théâtre was how Brick viewed his partnership with the beast. During one spell when money was tight at Chessington, he apparently pulled out his own gold fillings to buy meat for Habibi.

"Their relationship was quite extraordinary," wrote Edward Campbell, co-author of a later Brick biography. "Certain boundaries were laid down by tacit agreement. One of them was that Habibi was entitled to kill Brick if he could find a moment when his trainer's attention was less than continuous."

Given the way he perceived animals, it was perhaps inevitable that Brick followed the lead of others and began creating a gallery in the window of No. 40. For a man who had spent so little time in Germany, and none at all in the country when it was under Hitler's dark spell, to be taken from Habibi and others for political reasons was bizarre. Not to mention the personal trauma of being removed from beasts he regarded as his family, animals he knew would struggle to cope without the one human they trusted most.

Inscribing their likenesses on the painted window canvas was unquestionably a coping mechanism for somebody struggling with the pressure of being removed from his loved ones. One extant photograph shows him sitting proudly before his body of work, smiling for the camera with his creations over his shoulder.

His artistic endeavors aside, Brick was a gift to an incarcerated group of men battling to overcome boredom on a daily basis. Blessed by the presence of somebody who had led such an incredible life, they relished the chance to hear him dip into his bottomless fund of anecdotes and to share them with anybody interested. All of this explains why the eventual circumstances of his departure from Hutchinson have the dramatic whiff of legend.

By one account, Brick was released in the interest of public safety because the animals under his care could not be controlled without him there. By another, he simply applied to the authorities for his case to be reconsidered and it was established that he had no real affinity with Germany at all. Even after he had left, he still provided fodder for the men who remained behind barbed wire.

Witness the yarn spun about the circumstances of his reunion with Habibi.

According to the story, Brick returned to the zoo where Habibi had been housed in his absence only to find that the zookeeper refused to release the lion until he was recompensed for the food provided to the animal over the prior months. Completely broke after his stint at Hutchinson, Brick was in a quandary. Promised a job as animal wrangler on *The Dark Tower*, a movie about to go into production at Pinewood Studios, he needed his pet in order to start earning money again.

So, he returned to the zoo in the dead of night and levered open the cage where Habibi lay. He stared into the animal's eyes, reestablishing the long-standing bond between man and beast, and, after some nervous seconds, the lion walked toward him. Brick placed his whip around the animal's neck as a leash of sorts, and then the pair strode away into the night. By one account, he walked all the way to Pinewood in the dark, his lion striding next to him like a pet poodle. In another, he had a van waiting outside which he used to make his getaway.

For the men left behind at Hutchinson, either version of the tale sufficed to entertain them on the long winter nights when all that remained of Brick was his legend and his glass menagerie.

CHAPTER THREE

Degenerate Artists

The real reason for leaving Germany is this art form. It does not please Hitler who knows well how to put paint on the side of a barn but not how to put paint on canvas. He can see nothing in this.
—KURT SCHWITTERS, 1939

ON JULY 18, 1937, ADOLF HITLER FORMALLY OPENED THE NEWLY CONstructed House of German Art in Munich, and its inaugural show, "The Great German Art Exhibition." As the prominence of nationality in both titles indicates, there was a very specific purpose to the enterprise. As part of his determination to showcase what he considered to be the best of the Third Reich, he had charged three artists loyal to the regime with selecting works reflecting the values of the country he now led. When the original judges didn't meet with his approval quickly enough, his personal photographer Heinrich Hoffmann eventually came up with over nine hundred paintings that he knew the Führer would deem to be sufficiently, somehow quintessentially, German.

What did that mean, exactly? Well, it was in the eye of the beholder, perhaps easier defined by what the paintings *weren't* than by what they were. Anything by Jews, foreigners, or perceived Bolshevists was strictly prohibited. In a lengthy and typically bombastic speech he gave to mark the launch of the exhibit, Hitler was also unequivocal about the sort of stuff he now considered unsuitable for consumption by the German people. With all the pent-up frustration of a man who, in his youth, had twice failed to gain admission to the Vienna Academy of Art, he gave a lengthy soliloquy about the importance of art and the evils, in particular, of its most modern exponents.

"Art is in no way fashion," said Hitler. "In the same way that little changes in the nature and blood of our people, art, too, must lose its character of transience; instead, in its continuously intensifying creations, it must be a worthy visual expression of the life's course of our people. Cubism, Dadaism, Futurism, Impressionism, and so on, have nothing to do with our German people. For all of these terms are neither old nor modern, but are simply the stilted stammering of people to whom God has denied real artistic talent and has given instead the gift of blather and deception. I therefore wish to affirm in this hour my immutable resolve to do for German artistic life what I have done in the area of political confusion: to purge it of empty phrases."

Twenty-four hours later, he made good on his word. Across the street from the House of German Art, he walked into the Institute of Archaeology for an exhibition of *Entartete Kunst* (Degenerate Art). In the space of less than two weeks, his handpicked committee of regime-friendly arbiters stripped museums and galleries across Germany of 650 paintings, sculptures, and prints now deemed offensive to the aspirations of the Reich. In a space totally unsuitable for the purpose of displaying art—too dark and narrow, for starters—these works were situated, some-times haphazardly, and often deliberately without care.

The disdain for the pieces was in keeping with the mood of the times, for here was a showcase of everything Hitler and his cohorts believed had gone wrong with art since 1910, the cut-off point for selection. One mil-lion people would tramp through the doors over the following six weeks to look at the prohibited material that, beyond a who's who of German art of the era, also included works by foreign luminaries like Edvard Munch and Pablo Picasso. Some were there to scoff, others, privately no doubt, were there to discreetly marvel at the range and quality of these now strictly prohibited works.

There is a photograph taken of Hitler that opening day in which he is flanked by the men he had charged with hastily cobbling together this collection of what he regarded as anti-art. Alongside Heinrich Hoffmann, there's Professor Adolf Ziegler, his personal artistic adviser, and Wolfgang Willrich, an art critic and, like Hitler, another frustrated artist himself.

At one point, the camera catches Hitler laughing at a remark while standing in front of a wall on which paintings by Wassily Kandinsky, Paul Klee, and Kurt Schwitters are hanging, rather deliberately askew. Across the top of the display runs a quote from George Grosz that reads, "Take Dada seriously! It's worth it." All four artists were, in different ways, associated with the Dada movement, the Bauhaus, and so much that was innovative and memorable about the cultural renaissance of the Weimar Republic that predated Hitler's rise. Pointedly, by that juncture in German history, Grosz had emigrated to America, Kandinsky had fled to Paris, and Klee was living in Switzerland. All three had recognized that the specter of Nazism spelled the end for cultural freedoms and artistic expression and got out while they could.

As for Schwitters, in a less contentious time, he might have taken umbrage at being lumped in with the Dada movement. Although he undoubtedly shared some of its values, he was also careful to point out that he remained separate from the movement, too. Of course, these classification debates were trivialities from a different, more normal era. Now, under the new, strained, and strange circumstances, Hitler stood in front of their works, all housed together in a section titled *Total Verrückt*, which translated as "Completely Insane"—neatly capturing his view of the true artistic spirit of the time.

Schwitters had sixteen pieces in total on display in the *Entartete Kunst*, an indication of the prominence he had gained as an artist over the previous two decades. Like Grosz, Kandinsky, and Klee, he too had already fled Hitler's Germany by then. Six months before the exhibition opened, he gave up a rather comfortable upper-middle-class lifestyle for uncertain exile in Norway, a country he knew well and figured would be a temporary home until the Nazi madness abated. That wasn't to be the case.

Oslo turned into the first stop on a journey that ended at Hutchinson Camp, where, even in such exalted company, his reputation as an artist and his antics as an eccentric made him, in so many ways, the brightest light around the square. In the early days, when artistic materials were in scarce supply, Schwitters was undeterred. He'd spent much of his career advocating that just about anything could be turned into art, so scavenging in the most unlikely places came more naturally to him than it did to others. After breakfast each morning, he'd leave his own house and begin a walk around the square, stopping in every building to collect any still-warm porridge that had not been eaten by the residents. Once he had amassed as much as he could carry in his bucket, he returned to his own room to start sculpting with it.

Some appreciated his improvisational abilities more than others. The problem was that after a couple of days, the oatmeal sculptures tended to smell, growing mold and attracting rodents. That wasn't even the worst of it. On some occasions, they also started to melt and to drip down between the floorboards into the bedrooms of the men living below Schwitters, individuals for whom the glamour of sharing a house with an artistic genius soon wore off.

"Kurt Schwitters was our main star," said Freddy Godshaw, a fellow inmate. "Not only was he a world-famous artist, but he also was the most fascinating raconteur and could keep a full house entertained for hours. He wrote and recited a symphony in words. It lasted for fifteen to twenty minutes, and the musicians at the camp were most impressed. I have two sketches at home by Schwitters, one of my brother Walter and one of myself."

The Schwitters pieces were prized by the inmates because they knew well that if they ever got out of this place, those works were going to be worth something one day. Everything in his life up to then made that inevitable.

Kurt Hermann Eduard Karl Julius Schwitters was born on June 20, 1887, in the Saxony capital, Hanover, where his father Eduard and mother Henriette (nee Beckemeyer) ran a ladies' wear shop. The family was solidly middle class, with the means for him to travel to the 1900 World's Fair in Paris with his father.

"As a child I had a little garden with roses and strawberries in it," wrote Schwitters. "After I graduated from the *Realgymnasium* [scientific high school] in Hanover, I studied the technique of painting in Dresden with Bantzer, Kuhl, and Hegenbarth."

His decade of training in Dresden came to an end shortly after the outbreak of World War I. As an epileptic, Schwitters was originally exempt from military service, but when Germany needed more men, he enlisted and served his country for eighteen months, working as a drafts-man in a factory near Hanover. During the war, he also married Helma Fischer, a cousin. The couple moved into an apartment on the second floor of his parents' house and he commandeered a room on the first as a studio. After their first child Gerd died eight days after his birth in 1916, another son, Ernst, was born a week after the Armistice in 1918. It was that winter when Schwitters began experimenting with a more avant-garde approach to art.

"Because the medium is unimportant, I take any material whatsoever if the picture demands it," said Schwitters. "I play off material against material—for example, wood against sackcloth. I call the *weltanschauung* [worldview] from which this mode of artistic expression arose 'Merz.'"

The name was derived from a fragment of a word culled from a newspaper advertisement for the Kommerz bank, and it was to become an umbrella term to describe all strands of his extraordinary artistic out-put over the next two decades. Beyond exhibiting his avant-garde pieces as far away as America, he wrote plays, children's books, poems, and at least one screenplay, some of his best lines gleaned from eavesdrop-ping on conversations between passengers aboard trams and streetcars. Somewhere, in between all of that, he found time to make a living as a commercial artist, graphic designer, and, even, for five years, as official typographer for the Hanover town authorities.

He was busy at home, too, spending fourteen years creating *Merzbau*, a sculptural installation that eventually ended up stretching through two rooms and several balconies of the family home at Waldhausenstrasse 5. It incorporated pieces of art by his peers and all manner of found objects, reflecting his belief that every train ticket, shoelace, feather, dishcloth, or food wrapper had artistic potential. The *Merzbau* caused such a stir that photographs of it were exhibited at the Museum of Modern Art in New York in 1936.

"When he wasn't writing poems, he made collages," said Hans Richter, a peer and a friend, who offered a unique insight into Schwitters's chaotic approach to life and art. "If he wasn't occupied with gluing things, he worked on his column. He washed his feet in the same water where his guinea pigs bathed. He heated the pot with glue in his own bed; in the rarely used bathtub, he kept a tortoise. He recited, drew, cut printed magazines into pieces, welcomed guests, published *Merz* magazine, wrote letters, designed advertising prints for Gunter Wagner, gave drawing lessons, painted exceptionally bad portraits (he liked them), and cut them into pieces, which he later used in his abstract collage compositions. He assembled Merz compositions from broken furniture, nagged his wife to mind their sons, invited friends for very stingy dinners, and, among all that, he never forgot to pick [up] something from the ground and put it in his pocket."

Schwitters's rise to prominence as an artist during the 1920s and 1930s was backgrounded, of course, by the ominous ascent of the Nazi Party, a cloud beginning to overshadow every aspect of German society and culture. A matter of months after Hitler became chancellor, the German Press Association threw a banquet in Berlin. Schwitters happened to be staying in the city with the Hungarian artist and photographer Laszlo Moholy-Nagy and his wife Sybil. The trio went along to pay their respects to the visiting Italian writer, Filippo Tommaso Marinetti, author of *The Manifesto of Futurism*.

Marinetti was not the only big name present. A full roster of Nazi grandees was also there, including Joseph Goebbels, Ernst Röhm, Hermann Göring, and Rudolf Hess. While they sat together at the top table, lesser lights from the ruling party were seated around the room. Schwitters found himself between an official from the "Strength through Joy" movement, the body established to offer the working classes access to leisure and culture, and the leader of the National Socialist Organization for Folk Culture.

The wine flowed freely and, eventually, Schwitters couldn't resist engaging with the Nazis.

"I love you, you Cultural Folk and Joy," he said. "Honestly, I love you. You think I'm not worthy of sharing your chamber, your art chamber for strength and folk, but I'm an idiot, too, and I can prove it. You think I'm a Dadaist, don't you? That's where you're wrong, brother. I'm MERZ." He reiterated the point by smacking his hand over his heart. "I'm Aryan, the great Aryan MERZ. I can think Aryan, paint Aryan, spit Aryan. With this Aryan fist [now perilously close to the Nazi official's face], I shall destroy the mistakes of my youth."

Then he took a sip of his drink, shook his fist in front of their faces, and whispered, "If you want me to."

Schwitters was forty-six years old, making an excellent living from his various enterprises, and stealthily beavering away on the groundbreaking (literally and metaphorically) *Merzbau* at home. Even though the Nazi regime was only a few months old, haranguing minor Party officials in public was already a risky business. Moholy-Nagy intervened, put his hand on his friend's shoulder, and, without saying a word, persuaded him to stop talking.

At least temporarily. A few minutes later, he was off again.

"You will not prohibit me from Merzing my Merz art!" he roared, finally eliciting a response from the *petit fonctionnaire* from "Strength through Joy."

"Prohibited is prohibited," replied the Nazi, with emphasis on every word. "And when the Führer says 'Yes,' he says 'Yes,' and when he says 'No,' he says 'No.' Heil Hitler!"

That was enough to tip Schwitters over the edge.

Fortunately, his friends noticed as much and Marinetti decided to take evasive action. Rising to his feet, he announced to the room that he wished to regale them all with a recital of his poem, "The Raid on Adrianople." His dramatic soliloquy distracted the Nazis from the potential flashpoint and the rest of the evening passed without incident.

Like all artists, though, Schwitters was on notice that the country had changed irrevocably, and that their livelihoods—maybe even their very lives—were under real threat.

In the years following that contretemps, his son Ernst refused to be inducted into the Hitler Youth; Kate Steinitz, a friend and longtime collaborator, had been forced into exile; and the Nazi Party began officially describing some of Schwitters's work as "simply indescribable trash."

Against this tumultuous background, Schwitters began to consider his options in terms of leaving the country and finding a safe refuge. The Netherlands was briefly a possibility, until he realized it was prohibitively expensive. Norway was a more viable option because he had been spending time up there for years.

In July of 1929, he and Helma had traveled as far north as the island of Spitzbergen. Taken by the landscape, he returned to the northwest of the country every summer from 1931, usually staying in Djupvasshytta, a mountainous region not far from the Geiranger Fjord. Tourists visiting the area during that time often encountered him in hotel lobbies offering to do portraits of them for cash. A photograph taken by Ernst in that era captures his father outside a log cabin in the hills, standing before an easel with an umbrella over the canvas and clouds scudding by in the background. The portrait of an artist at work. At peace.

The prospect of decamping full-time to a country where he enjoyed such productive sojourns became a more urgent matter in August of 1936 when the Gestapo arrested Christof Spengemann, his friend and publisher, along with his wife Luise and son Walter. Ernst Schwitters, by then eighteen, had toiled alongside the Spengemanns in the SF—the Sozialistische Front, an anti-Nazi left-wing party—and he fled north to Norway the day after Christmas 1936. His father, who may have done some low-level courier work for the SF, waited less than a week before taking the same path out of Germany. Days after his departure, a letter arrived from the Gestapo requesting him to come in for an interview.

"But I did not want to emigrate," claimed Schwitters. "I only wanted to come a week later with the things that Ernst could not take with him and stay there two months to help him set up."

Helma did not make a permanent move from Hanover but did travel up for extended visits to Lysaker, just outside of Oslo, where the Schwitters men set up residence. While the family began stealthily trying to relocate some of his major works from Germany to Norway, Schwitters embarked on the production of two new *Merzbau*—the first, in Haus am Bakken (House on the Slope) in Lysaker; and the second, in his summer cottage on the island of Hjertøya, near Molde.

As the world seemed to be tumbling inexorably into war, Schwitters just kept working. While the nature of his output changed—there were far more landscapes and portraits than before—the three years that he lived in Norway appear to have been among his most fecund periods. The productivity of a man hitting the prime of his artistic life, or somebody driven by the knowledge that civilization appeared to be on the brink of lurching toward disaster?

The prolific run was interrupted because the latter prospect suddenly appeared frighteningly real when German troops invaded Norway on April 9, 1940. The period of idyllic exile came to an abrupt halt, artistic matters being quickly put aside, as staying out of the Gestapo's grasp now became the family's number one priority. With Ernst and his new wife Esther as traveling companions, Schwitters fled north by train to evade the onrushing Nazi forces.

"The very next day, as they reached Molde, German troops arrived at their abandoned apartment in the suburb of Lysaker, where they burned books and several pictures but left the Haus am Bakken intact," wrote Megan R. Luke in her biography of Schwitters. "When they were barred by the police from rowing out to their hut on the island of Hjertøya, the family made their way to the port of Ålesund, a short way south along the coast, where they were quickly interned as prisoners of war with captured German soldiers in the neighboring town of Skodje to the east. Upon their release, they attempted to return to Molde; when they arrived at the port of Vestnes, they could see their destination up in flames across the bay. At this moment, Schwitters knew they would have to leave Norway entirely."

From there, Kurt, Ernst, and Esther caught a fishing boat north. They reached the Lofoten Islands, passing through Sortland, Kabelvag, and Horstad, where they were again detained by the authorities. This desperate journey paralleled that of the Norwegian king and his government at the same time. By June 8, the Schwitters family was in Tromso, their quest to escape the clutches of the Nazis taking them deep into the Arctic Circle. There, they tried to board the *Fridtjof Nansen*, an icebreaker that was full of evacuees. According to one account, they were only allowed on because Halvdan Koht, Norway's minister for foreign affairs, knew Ernst from Lysaker and intervened on their behalf.

The elder Schwitters remained eerily calm as they huddled together, waiting for the final order to board the ship. With sirens wailing and Nazi aircraft patrolling the skies above them, Kurt took three white mice from his pocket and let them roam free before chasing them down. Later, he told his fellow passengers that he had used the rodents to distract himself from the frightening situation at hand. The *Fridtjof Nansen* turned out to be the last civilian ship to leave the port; within forty-eight hours of its departure, the Germans had complete control of Norway.

Schwitters still had one white mouse in his pocket when the *Fridtjof Nansen* reached the Scottish port of Leith after ten days at sea. He and his son and daughter-in-law soon learned that their joy at once more avoiding the Gestapo was to be short-lived. The British authorities classified them as "enemy aliens," and over the next month they did the circuit of the various internment camps, staying at Midlothian, Edinburgh, York Racecourse, and the dreaded Warth Mills (where Ernst had a typewriter stolen) before they boarded another boat and arrived on the Isle of Man on July 17, 1940. As Schwitters's file was being processed at Hutchinson Camp, under "Normal Occupation," the officials wrote "portrait painter"; under "Present Occupation," they wrote "nil."

As an art historian, Klaus Hinrichsen knew of Schwitters's work; indeed, he had seen some of it displayed in the "Degenerate Art" exhibition back in 1937. Yet he didn't recognize the artist until the writer Richard Friedenthal introduced Klaus to a rather conservatively dressed gentleman in a buttoned-up, gray-striped, three-piece suit, replete with sober tie, announcing, "The great Dadaist Kurt Schwitters." The character standing before him was not what he'd envisaged a daring, innovative artist would look like.

"He looked a typical German *bürger*, and could easily have been mistaken for a highly respectable small-town businessman immersed in local affairs," said Hinrichsen. "Only two things upset this *bürger* image: the fact he wore no socks in his boots (he never did!); and the slender piece of wood in his hand which he was shaping with a pocketknife into some abstract design."

That strip of birch wood had been in his possession all through their perilous flight through Norway. When the mood took him, he had sculpted it into shape, and one of the first sights many of his inmates caught of him at the new camp was Schwitters sitting on a bench, pecking and slicing at the Norwegian wood that became the first completed work of this new stage of his life.

Schwitters asked Hinrichsen to give him a tour of the camp so he could get acquainted with the layout. As the pair of them strolled along, he noticed the artist kept his head down as they walked and talked, better to spot any interesting litter or detritus that might be reconstituted as art. Their amble culminated at the top of the square, a vantage point where the streets slope downward and which, once you ignored the double rows of barbed-wire perimeter, offered a spectacular view over the roofs of Douglas, the harbor below, and, in the distance, the Irish Sea.

"As soon as I can lay my hands on some canvas and paint, I shall paint this," said Schwitters.

In fact, he was to devote more time to painting portraits than anything else in the camp because it made economic sense. Arriving in Britain with no money and just the baggage he could carry, he was desperate for cash, and soon turned himself into an artist for hire by those internees who had money in their pockets when they were swept up.

"I can see him slouching along the street in a green loden suit," says Freddy Godshaw. "He stopped me in the street and insisted on doing it. It only took him a few minutes. He charged so much for a head, so much for head and shoulders, so much for full-length. But he didn't charge us [his brother Walter was also in the camp], as he knew our father from Hanover."

For those with no familial connection, the going rate for a portrait was £3 for a head, £4 for a head and shoulders, and £5 for head, shoulders, arms, and hands. Schwitters knew he enjoyed a reputation that had commercial value even behind barbed wire. Eventually, he was making enough from his hustling to purchase cigars and wine to improve his quality of life at Hutchinson. His cause was also helped by the fact that Commander Daniel was quite taken with having an avant-garde icon under his care, and his fulsome appraisal of Schwitters caused many of the British officers to commission him to do their portraits. Never mind that he was now producing work far removed from the type of collages that made him one of the great Modernists of the era just a few years earlier.

For all of his mercenary approach to improving his precarious financial state, Schwitters was not the type to absent himself from camp life. He threw himself into the hustle and bustle and, sifting through the testimonies of his fellow residents about their experiences, there is an argument to be made that he was often the most entertaining character in the place, a competitive enough category, that.

"Schwitters tells his marvellous stories," wrote Fred Uhlman, of seeing him light up the camp one September day. "'How the bed bugs came into the Royal Academy at Hanover,' the black, beautiful 'glass' which he discovered and . . . left on the hot oven, the poisoned mushrooms which he ate. After the talk he gave me a short story which he had written for me entitled, 'The Story of the Flat and Round Painter.'"

A few weeks later, Uhlman went to sit for Schwitters, who was working on a portrait of him. By that point, the most celebrated artist in camp had been afforded his own private attic space, a recognition by Commander Daniel of his emeritus status even in such exalted company. As Uhlman approached the house, he heard dogs barking—an alien sound, since pets of any kind were strictly prohibited in Hutchinson. But what else could it be?

Upon entering the lobby of the building, he got his answer. There, he found a Viennese businessman doing his best impression of an angry canine while several floors above, the redoubtable Schwitters responded, as if the pair were enjoying a perfectly reasonable exchange of views, albeit in dog language.

" 'Woo, woo, woo, woo,' barked the Viennese as fast as he could," wrote Uhlman. " 'Woo—woo—woo,' answered Schwitters from the top landing, but not half as fast as the Viennese dachshund, more like an elderly, well-mannered Alsatian. 'Woo, woo, woo, woo, woo, woo, woo,' yelled the dachshund. 'Woo—woo—woo,' came the dignified reply. This went on for at least five minutes. Then both dogs retired, each to his room."

In Schwitters's attic, he had gone full method actor with the dog stuff, converting his table into a kennel of sorts. He had blankets hanging over the sides of the table and his mattress was underneath. Like a good doggie, he sidled in there to the darkness and safety at night, usually after some more therapeutic bedtime barking to relieve his stress. While his eccentric living arrangement gave his housemates and fellow artists plenty to talk about, Schwitters also gave lectures about art history, amusing the audience when describing Picasso as a "gangster."

Although one of the more learned professors derided his best literary efforts as "infantile poetry," that seems to have been a minority opinion. Again and again, he lifted the mood of his fellow internees with the various strands of his multifaceted cabaret act, and decades later, many still testified to Schwitters making them laugh even on their darkest days with his ridiculous party pieces.

"So once a cup or a saucer was broken, this was disaster in the camp," said Hinrichsen. "And one of Schwitters's great performances was to take a cup and a saucer and slowly move it in front of him, in his hand, and say 'silence, silence, silence,' and get louder and louder and turn this cup on the saucer quicker and quicker and suddenly he would scream 'silence,' throw the cup into the air, hit it with the saucer, and both would fall onto the floor broken. Now at that time this was sacrilege and really quite unforgettable. When I now see a broken cup or saucer I still have to think that Schwitters broke it, as he broke them in the camp."

If his disregard for the camp crockery and willingness to smash it in the quest for a gag improved the mood of many of the internees, his impact on their language was even more pronounced. Many were so taken by his performances of the *Ursonate*, a sonata in primordial sounds which he had released on a 78 rpm vinyl record back in 1932, that they began to mimic it. Having heard the distinctive and discordant sound poem so often, they began to use phrases from it when greeting each other around the square.

"Lanke trrgll," said the first man.

"Pi pi pi ooka ooka zueka zueka," said his friend.

For all the joy he was bringing to those with whom he shared space, Schwitters was battling demons of his own. The cheery persona and vaudevillian antics disguised a man privately struggling, like so many others, with the imposition of exile.

"Christmas—and I am a prisoner," he wrote on Christmas Eve, 1940, in a letter to Helma. "It is a trial. I went to our church, unable to believe in man's love for his fellow man. The traditional carols were sung. I could not sing. I see my goal in art and I learn to hate people."

CHAPTER FOUR

A Welfare State

It is my wish that every man who enters internment on the island shall be assured that nothing avoidable will be done that might add to his discomfort or unhappiness. . . . A man's internment is not regarded here as a reflection on his character. He is credited with being a man of good intent until he proves himself otherwise. . . . The measure of your co-operation and good behavior will decide the measure of your privilege and the consideration shown for your welfare.
—LIEUTENANT-COLONEL S. W. SLATTER, COMMANDANT, ISLE OF MAN CAMPS, JUNE 1, 1940

AT NO. 7 HUTCHINSON SQUARE, THE COOK WAS MR. WEINER, A schoolteacher from Berlin so masterful in the kitchen that every other resident was expected to put in a shift doing the prep work before the culinary master worked his magic. One task of the support staff included trudging to the top of the square each morning to collect the food rations provided; another was cleaning the herrings, a thankless job Fritz Hallgarten was especially squeamish about. When his turn on the roster came around, he complained and often beseeched one of his colleagues to fill in for him.

"Nobody there would do it for me," he said. "But one day somebody shouted, 'I'd do it for a shilling,' and I said, 'All right.'"

That night, a huge argument ensued in the house about the ethics and morality of what he had done. Some called his gesture in hiring

43

a fellow inmate undemocratic, while others argued that it was just an inevitable by-product of a group of men living together and sharing space. Hallgarten's own stance was simple enough. By paying a less well-off neighbor to deal with the fish, he enabled that man (who didn't like to receive charity) to do something to earn some extra cash. And this outsourcing of a task he despised also freed him up to get to his more important job—heading up the camp's welfare office, a role in which he was working on behalf of every resident.

The very existence of a welfare office spoke to the way in which Commander Daniel and the internees had quickly put together an ad hoc system of government, replete with the structures of a society.

"I was the minister for welfare, what the commandant called the representative of the destitute," said Hallgarten. "First of all, I got money from the commander to give one shilling a week to the destitute prisoners to buy cigarettes or socks or boots. If they needed anything I noted it down and they signed a receipt once the stuff came in. Within the camp, you couldn't distinguish the destitute from the others, they were just as well dressed, but they were wearing army boots, supplied by my office. If they needed other things there was no difference. I had to look after people so they were looking after themselves, I was a social worker."

In common with every other resident, Hallgarten's career had once been on a very different path. As a law student in Frankfurt in the early 1920s, he joined the Kartell-Convent der Verbindungen deutscher Studenten jüdischen Glaubens, the society of Jewish fraternities better known simply as Kartell-Convent, or KC. Established in 1886 when a wave of anti-Semitism led to the exclusion of Jews from existing campus fraternities in Germany, the association believed in evincing honor in the face of religious discrimination and prided itself on fighting back. By the time Hallgarten signed up in the early 1920s, the KC was doing battle with a nascent threat called National Socialism.

"In 1923, my fraternity was fully mobilized to fight Hitler if he succeeded in his putsch in Munich," said Hallgarten. "We were prepared to start a civil war to fight him down. We were very active. As an organization we went to small villages in Hessen and entered Nazi meetings to disrupt them. We split up to ask questions to disrupt and to show opposition to speakers, to draw attention to the fact there was opposition."

Hallgarten and his comrades used to tell a joke about Hitler addressing a meeting.

"The Jews are to blame," Hitler shouts.

"Not only the Jews," says a voice from the audience. "Also the cyclists."

"Why the cyclists?" asks Hitler.

"Why the Jews?" comes the reply.

By the time Hitler gained power in 1933, the time for joking was over. Hallgarten was now a junior member of Reichsbund jüdischer Frontsoldaten, an organization formed by Jewish soldiers who had fought for Germany in World War I. He had been too young to serve, but his father wore the uniform in that conflict. As the Nazi menace grew larger, Hallgarten attended many clandestine meetings. His presence at these events, and his previous decade of involvement with political groups opposed to the present Führer, brought him to the attention of the new authorities.

At this stage in his life a prominent lawyer who had also enjoyed a stint as an auxiliary judge in Frankfurt, Hallgarten's flourishing legal career was ended by a menacing instruction to stay away from the courthouse. For his own safety. Hallgarten pleaded his case with the president of the court, aided by the partner in his practice, but was told that there was a revolution afoot, and he was never to return to the building. That was only the beginning of his troubles. After being seen tearing down Nazi posters, he was forced into hiding on April 1, 1933.

Bizarrely, Hallgarten ended up spending some of his time on the run with relatives of Hermann Göring, the founder of the Gestapo. The Görings had once been on the opposing side to clients of his in a court case and, when the financial terms of the settlement were prohibitive, Hallgarten had offered a compromise that spared them going broke. At the time, they assured him that if he ever needed help he only had to ask. They were as good as their word, but by July 1, Hallgarten was in England, choosing it over France because his wife Frieda had an aunt who had married an Englishman and had been there for years.

At that point in the still young decade, Hallgarten met many English people who didn't quite understand what was going on in Germany, failing to comprehend exactly why he had to flee his native country. Some wondered if he was on the run for some sort of crime, and didn't even grasp the issue when he explained that being Jewish had, essentially, become an offense against the Nazi state. His younger brother Otto ended up being arrested and imprisoned in Esterwegen, one of the first concentration camps in Germany. It took bribery and exploiting every political connection the family had to secure Otto's release and eventually get him to London, too.

Unable to practice law in England, Hallgarten's options were so limited that he was advised to explore chicken farming, a profession he knew nothing about. He did have some experience with grapes, though, having regularly helped his father, who dabbled in the wine industry, even filling in for him when he was off fighting for the Kaiser. Eleven months after arriving in London, Hallgarten set himself up as a wine importer, funded by a loan from his father-in-law and believing there was a gap in the English market for more European wines.

Shortly before war broke out, he applied for British citizenship. That, and the fact he had supplied the authorities with crucial information about German plans to build a new airstrip, counted for little when internment began. Together with his friend Ronald Stent (see chapter 7), he was taken in the early morning from his cottage in Kings Langley, and from there to Bertram Mills, Ascot Racecourse, Kempton Park, and eventually, to the Isle of Man. Upon arriving at Hutchinson Square he noticed that there was a very famous wine merchant on the corner of a nearby street. A reminder of the life he had left behind.

Aside from showing how well run the facility was, the existence of a welfare office spoke to the fact that Commander Daniel and his staff realized the internees were a cross section of society at large, boasting men from every demographic. There were some wealthy characters—a sprinkling of industrialists, such as Richard Cohn (who formerly owned a chain of shoe stores), and G. Hirschmann (proprietor of a flourishing brick factory in Breslau). But there was also a large swathe who arrived with very little cash, and, crucially, also lacked the outside connections to get friends and family to mail them money or parcels of clothing or other goods.

That was where Hallgarten came in. Perhaps his previous stint as a judge gave the impression that here was somebody who would be fair and just in administering funds to those in need.

"There were also others in the camp who helped people," he said. "If somebody had no cigarettes, there were always people willing to give them cigarettes, because, remember, there were some people in the camp who were very rich. They were quite willing to give to other people."

Again, the nature of the debate when Hallgarten effectively hired a housemate to do his most distasteful kitchen shift shows a group of men contending with the strictures of a community created under strained circumstances. In an obvious effort to bridge the gap between the haves and have-nots, Daniel introduced a measure restricting internees from withdrawing more than ten shillings a week from the camp bank. Of course, it didn't take long for somebody to figure out a loophole that could be exploited.

Some wealthier men reckoned this was a tad unfair, as the allowed sum was barely enough if an individual wanted to pay for laundry, tobacco, shoe repair, or extra food. They soon figured out an easy way around the rule. Departing prisoners were allowed to cash out their balance at the bank, and those staying behind wrote them checks so they could get their hands on more money inside the barbed wire.

Aside from ensuring the more mendicant internees were looked after, Hallgarten's position also came with other unofficial responsibilities. Many came to his door hoping to tap into his expertise as a lawyer, bringing queries about family law as men dealt with divorce or separation and the needs of wives and children on the outside. Occasionally, he was also roped into sorting out heavyweight theological conundrums, including a case where an Orthodox Jewish internee had received his release papers on the grounds that he would sail out of Liverpool for America on Yom Kippur.

"You can be on the high seas on the highest holiday but you cannot start the journey on the highest holiday," said Hallgarten. "The rabbis asked laymen and lawyers, including me, for my opinion, and we all agreed it was a question of saving life. If he doesn't go now, will he ever get the seat on a boat again? We decided he should go, and he went."

Hallgarten was present for two official visits from the Home Office. The first was led by Osbert Peake, the under-secretary of state, who embarked on something of a goodwill tour, wanting to see that the internees were being treated properly and urging the men to show patience as his department worked its way through evaluating each individual's case for release. The arrival of T. B. Angliss, the Home Office liaison and welfare officer from the headquarters of the alien internment camps in Douglas, prompted a much more thorough investigation of how the camp was run and how internees were conducting themselves.

When Angliss knocked on the door of the welfare office, he wanted a forensic accounting of every man who had received financial assistance and whether they had been given money, shoes, or underwear. These were statistics and records Hallgarten had kept so rigorously that even the civil servant was impressed.

"Did you have some clerical education before you came to the camp?" he asked.

"None whatsoever," said Hallgarten. "I was a wine importer in the city of London."

"What has happened to your company?"

"My brother is looking after my affairs."

"Oh, I'm sure he is much older than you."

"No, he's younger."

"I'm sure he's been here longer."

"No, he came here four years later than me."

"Why hasn't he been interned?" asked Angliss.

"Why have I been interned?" asked Hallgarten.

While Angliss left without saying anything directly to Hallgarten about the remark, Hallgarten was asked to report to Daniel's office the next day. There, he was reprimanded for having the temerity to speak like that to an official of the Home Office, a representative of His Majesty's government. He listened to the rebuke but stood his ground, pointing out that he was allowed to argue his point because "I was still on the same level as Mr. Angliss and was still free to speak in a free country, even if behind barbed wire."

As demonstrated by Hallgarten's smooth operating of the welfare office, Commander Daniel wanted his facility to be an exemplar to all others on the island.

"In all our efforts both inside and outside the wire, it must be our constant aim to keep going and never flag in our united efforts to make our camp perfect," he wrote in the first issue of *The Camp* newspaper. "I would like to add that the loyal backing received from the Camp Father, and Assistant Camp Fathers, supported by the House Fathers, has made my work a pleasure, and the hard work carried on behind the scenes by all Camp Departments and Clerical Workers is also fully appreciated by my fellow officers. . . . Let me impress upon every one of you your duty to your fellow men to carry out with cheerfulness and alacrity any service you may be called upon to do. Let the Camp's motto be 'Happiness in Co-Operation!'"

Daniel had put in place a pyramidical system of government designed to give every resident a voice. Each building had to elect a House Father whose job it was to represent his roommates and to report back to them from meetings with the authorities. Each row of houses then elected a Row or Street Father, and above that level reigned an overall Camp Father. The idea was to give the men a vested interest in camp affairs, and more than one internee remarked that the setup was similar to how the British had once ruled India with the assistance of the local rajas.

The system was also designed so inmates wouldn't go directly to the authorities with a complaint. They first had to raise it with their House Father and then move it up along the chain of command. Obviously, the Camp Father, regarded as a sort of higher power, was the most influential figure, the person who dealt most often with the commander. The first man to hold the position was Rudolph Munster, a lawyer from Westphalia whose wife Ruth was from Manchester.

"Well, above all I had to sort out the organization, to get it practically going," said Munster. "I was the one who was invited to the British administration if any orders had to be given, which was to start with, more frequent. And I had to work together with them. Which I did. The commandant [Daniel] was a charming man. He was a sort of a bit of a sergeant-major, but he had a good heart. We often talked about things. This was my job, and I tried to make him understand what was going on there. . . . But, of course, when he gave an order, we were under military command, you really had to obey."

Munster's elevation to the role had been on the whim of a British army officer who, on the ship going to the Isle of Man, had identified him as somebody capable of getting the rest of the passengers into order. Thereafter, however, every resident got to vote in an election to decide who should be the Camp Father, and four different men (Munster, Friedrich Burschell, Paul Henning, and Dr. Brückmann) filled the position in the first six months of the camp's existence.

The departure of Henning—a photographer who produced some stunning linocut portraits of the square during his time at the camp—prompted an anonymous article in *The Camp* newspaper about some of the men who held the office, and offered an interesting take on the contribution of Dr. Brückmann, the erstwhile Deputy Camp Father who had just been elected to the top job.

"Since more than a quarter of a year, this position has been held by Dr. Brückmann," went the report. "He was never much popular, he was attacked by many people—but everybody without exception acknowledged his zeal, his hard [work] and correct conducting [of] the functions of his position. It was fully justified to nominate him for the free post of Camp Father—and his election may be understood as a kind of reward for his former doings. As the new Camp Father, his obligations are of more representative a sort; the spade work will be done in future by the former Street Father, Mr. Simmel, his deputy."

The men in these positions were the buffer between the disgruntled internees and the authorities, their job to hear every complaint and grumble and then to bring these issues to the attention of Commander Daniel.

"Your role really was that much more of a father than a captain because, you know, the powers were very limited," said Hinrichsen, House Father of No. 19 at just twenty-seven years of age. "Your powers were to be the father confessor, to listen to people, and to try to solve their problems. You certainly were a father to the younger ones and that was really hard.... If you don't make too many blunders and you behave reasonably, okay, they accept you. They expect too much, obviously, because as I said, your powers are so limited. You can't do a thing. All you can hope for is keeping the peace in the house, and doing the roll call in the morning."

Morning and evening roll call was a staple of any internment camp. However, the recordkeeping at Hutchinson in this regard tended toward the laissez-faire. Even though all men were commanded to present themselves outside the house for a formal head count, it was often a haphazard affair, especially at eight a.m., when a few came rushing out of the house half-dressed to fulfill their duty. Sometimes, individuals who were unwell, or just being recalcitrant, refused to get out of bed altogether. And then there were the complications created by some rather unpronounceable German names.

"We had to stand sleepy-eyed outside our house," said Ronald Stent. "The sergeant-major [Potterton], a typical Cockney, had to call the roll and it was a tongue-twister with the names of all these people. And he made mincemeat out of those names, and we were such an undisciplined lot. Three times he went through the names; he had assistance, three times. He could never get the correct number."

On occasion one of the soldiers would assist the sergeant-major by walking into a house to find the missing person and verify they were actually in bed, and hadn't escaped. The rest of the men found this hilarious because the prospect of somebody trying to leave a camp where they were so well treated was ludicrous. It says much for the "security" concerns that Hinrichsen was able to tell three newcomers to stay in bed one morning because their journey to the Isle of Man had wiped them out, promising to explain their absence to the sergeant-major. Who, presumably, took his word for it.

The Camp Fathers were all consulted when it came to the efforts made to improve residents' quality of life. Over the course of the first summer, builders constructed a communal shower facility on the north side of the square. When it finally opened, the men had plenty to say about its operation. There were complaints about how difficult it was to wash oneself while having one hand pulling on the water chain at all times, gripes about the grate in the drain being wide enough for the soap to fall through, and moans about the cool breeze that blew through the dressing rooms.

In early October, the commander announced another positive development he believed might make living in the camp more tolerable.

"It has been decided to install a loudspeaker connection in all houses and further agreed that a weekly sum of 1d (the equivalent of a couple of cents) per head for each internee be charged to cover costs," wrote Daniel. "This fund will be administered by the Finance Committee, and after establishing a sufficient reserve the balance will be passed to the Destitute Fund. The Programme which will emanate from the Control Room at headquarters will embrace the BBC News, music, and as varied a programme as possible.

"It will also be possible to make announcements of general interest to the camp. Each house will have its loudspeaker with Tone Control and also it will be possible to turn off the set independently by houses when not required. It is felt that with the long winter evenings fast approaching this new acquisition to our Camp will prove a great blessing and contribute to everybody's enjoyment."

Daniel's innovations suggest that he was keenly aware of the needs and wants of his internees. However, the men of Hutchinson were routinely baffled when he took to the microphone and delighted in delivering the scores of cricket matches being played around the country. Even for those who spoke fluent English, this was a foreign tongue describing an alien sport. Nobody cared.

When Bertha Bracey, chairman of the Central Department for Interned Refugees and General-Secretary of the German Emergency Committee of the Society of Friends, visited the camp, she wrote a piece for *The Guardian*, marveling at how the public address service could be turned on and off in each individual room. The arrival of the loudspeakers was accompanied by another announcement the same week, making beer available in the canteen—albeit under restricted circumstances. Each internee was allowed to have only one pint per day and a warning was issued that failing to adhere to that particular regulation would lead to the alcohol being withdrawn from the fare on offer.

Daniel and his cohorts seemed determined to provide as good a quality of life as possible under the strained circumstances. A nearby sports field had been commandeered for use by the internees. A group of men were brought from the camp to play football there, and were determined to be all-inclusive in terms of attracting new recruits.

"We ask all friends of the game to join us on our training, daily 10:30 a.m., provided the weather is fair," wrote Otto Mark in a notice inviting players. "We intend also to have training sometimes at 3:45 p.m., after special announcements. Meeting place is at the gate. We hope to see more and more people interested in football which can be played very well even by not so young gentlemen. It is intended to form a 'Senior— Eleven.' All footballers and friends of this game are asked to report with me in house 23, as well as people interested in handball and ping-pong."

Some men liked to jog around the perimeter of the lawn in the center of the square. Others did PT (physical training) workouts on the grass or played an improvised sport alternatively referred to as handball, or fistball. There were even a few boxing dilettantes who enjoyed sparring sessions outside, and, following the construction of a hall, indoors, too.

Eventually, once it had been established that none of the internees were a serious escape risk, the commander introduced excursions beyond the barbed wire. When the weather allowed, any interested men could walk down the hill under armed guard to the waterfront in order to take a swim. For some, it was a wonderful break from the monotony of the routine. For others, not so much.

"I never left the camp for walks or to go swimming because I said I would only leave as a free man," said Fritz Hallgarten. "I never left the camp, never went bathing. You could go once or twice a week. Everybody went out but I sat there with one or two older men who didn't want to go into the cold water. Everybody went out because they were pleased to get out of the camp. They went under guard, always guards, and that's why I wouldn't go. I would have been under guard by men with weapons. I wouldn't join for that."

Outings to the cinema also became an entertainment option. Indeed, accounts of those trips to the movies contain references to a lax security presence, something that made the inmates who did venture out very happy. So did newsreel footage of German setbacks in the war, something they cheered lustily during every visit. The degree of trust Daniel had invested in the men over time was such that on one occasion, an internee fell asleep in the theater and had to make his own leisurely way back to the camp when he woke up. Upon reaching the gate in the barbed wire, the guards didn't believe his story and initially refused him reentry.

Like Hallgarten, Hellmuth Weissenborn was another conscientious objector to any trip outside the camp, refusing all invitations to the beach or the theater, as long as there were soldiers with bayonets involved. He did relent, however, when the director of the Manx Museum issued a special invitation for him to spend a day at the facility. Even though Daniel insisted he be accompanied by an armed guard, Weissenborn decided just this once that it was worth it.

While Daniel took great pride in a camp where relations with the internees were mostly good, there were still occasional flashpoints. The postal system was a constant bugbear. Aside from the fact that internees were allowed to write only two letters per week, restricted to twenty-four lines each on prepared paper, there was the interminable wait for incoming missives from wives and family members on the outside, often writing to report on the latest of ongoing attempts to secure their release. More urgently, some internees were also receiving gifts of money in the mail.

As tightly run as Daniel hoped his ship was, there were logistical difficulties. From August onward, complaints started to filter through from residents and their wives that packages sent by registered mail were not reaching the men of Hutchinson Square.

On July 18, 1940, Emilie Neuberger sent a registered letter containing a £1 note to her husband, Dr. Eugen Neuberger, who had just arrived at Hutchinson. He never received the letter or the money.

On August 9, Elizabeth Liebermann sent a registered letter containing £5 to her husband, Dr. Max Liebermann. He never received the letter or the money. When her local postmaster at Leatherhead in Surrey investigated, he discovered that the letter had reached the camp, and a receipt was given for it.

Nine days later, Ida Lambek sent a registered letter from London containing £2 to her husband, Dr. Chaim Lambek, at No. 12. He never received the letter or the money, even though her local post office confirmed that it had reached the island and was delivered to the camp on August 20. A Private A. Clements had signed for it, and that signature was in the book.

To lose one letter would be understandable in the chaos of wartime Britain. To lose three, all of which contained cash, in the space of a few weeks looked more sinister. It was October before the missing mail came to the attention of Daniel, who presumably would have known that many of the residents had, in their various stops en route to the island, been angered at losing valuables to thieving guards at the more transitory camps.

"It was ascertained that two bags of registered mail had been signed for by Sgt. Heime on the 18th and 29th August respectively, but were not shown in the records kept," wrote Daniel in a report to the Home Office. "Sgt. Heime was questioned as to the disposal of the bags in question, and stated that he would have given the bags unopened to an orderly to be handed to the Intelligence Department, where they would have been opened, and the internees' letters entered in a register kept for that purpose."

To ensure that this didn't happen again, Daniel changed the system immediately so that the accounts department was given sole authority and responsibility for signing for and giving receipts for registered mail. By that point, however, there were sixty-five letters unaccounted for, all of which had contained either treasury notes, postal orders, or cash, a significant enough number for the authorities beyond Hutchinson to get involved, especially when the wives of those interned sought compensation. In her own letter to the Home Office, Emilie Neuberger pointed out, "The loss of one pound would be a considerable misfortune in our situation."

In a way that spoke to the rigor with which he wanted the camp to be run, Daniel provided a full accounting of every letter that failed to reach its destination, including the name of the sender, the would-be recipient, and the sums involved. He even reported that Dr. Bruno Kahn failed to receive a Parker fountain pen, value 17 and 6 (about $40 in today's money), that had been sent to him by a Miss G. Farner.

"Briefly the facts are that a private soldier, I believe one of the AMPC [Auxiliary Military Pioneer Corps], was found to be untrustworthy and sent from the Camp," wrote T. B. Angliss, reporting on the issue to the Home Office. "He was employed partly in the Orderly Room and signed for some of the registered letters. There is a mass of correspondence with the Post Office in the matter which [Commander] Daniels [*sic*] can tell you all about, but there is a matter of twenty-one pounds missing, and it is, I think, the worry of an otherwise well-ordered camp."

CHAPTER FIVE

The Spirit of the Camp

*Germany today is in a state of barbarism. The dictatorship knows
no law, it does not even respect its own. It maintains law courts
and prisons, but at the same time it runs concentration camps. Any
administrative act can be examined before the Supreme Administrative Court, but not the deeds of the Secret State Police, for which it
denied jurisdiction. The State has its authorities, but where these are
"insufficient," the Party will intervene.*
—RUDOLF OLDEN, *HITLER, THE PAWN,* 1935

THE SS *CITY OF BENARES* DEPARTED LIVERPOOL FOR THE CANADIAN
ports of Quebec and Montreal on Friday, September 13, 1940. Stretching a smidgen over 386 feet, boasting three steam turbines that made
it capable of reaching a top speed of 15 knots, it was part of OB 213, a
nineteen-vessel convoy accompanied on the initial leg of the transatlantic
voyage by a Royal Navy destroyer, the HMS *Winchelsea,* and two sloops.
With a crew of over 200, among the 197 passengers on board were 90
children being evacuated from England as part of the Children's Overseas Reception Board (CORB) scheme.

The threat of attack by a German U-boat was so omnipresent that in
the first few days of the journey, passengers were regularly drilled about
the lifeboat evacuation procedure and instructed to sleep in their life
jackets. As was normal on these perilous trips, Captain Landles Nicoll
was zigzagging his way out into the Atlantic Ocean to avoid detection,

his crew avidly watching the skies for enemy spotter planes. On September 17, the weather had deteriorated so much that the *Benares* and the other ships stopped taking evasive action. By then, the HMS *Winchelsea* had turned back to escort a vessel traveling in the other direction, bringing much-needed supplies from the United States to Britain.

Thirty-year-old Kapitänleutnant Heinrich "Ajax" Bleichrodt had taken command of the German submarine U-48 the previous month. On September 15, his first patrol in the Atlantic, he sank two British ships and a Greek steamer, beginning a war record that would culminate in him receiving the Knight's Cross of the Iron Cross with Oak Leaves, and eventually having a nervous breakdown at sea. Two days after his first foray, U-48 was six hundred miles west of the Hebrides when Bleichrodt spotted the now defenseless *City of Benares* in open water. Waiting for darkness to come, Bleichrodt finally gave the order to fire two torpedoes fifteen minutes before midnight. Both failed to hit the target.

The clock had just ticked into September 18 when U-48 dispatched another torpedo. This one tore through the *Benares* at the stern, underneath the children's quarters. After the shock of the initial explosion, the frenzied attempt at evacuation began. Fifty-five-year-old Rudolf Olden and his wife Ika, thirty-five, were asleep in their bunk when the boat was struck. A renowned lawyer and journalist in Weimar Germany, a former professor at Oxford University, and, most recently, an inmate of and esteemed lecturer at Hutchinson Camp, he was en route to take up a teaching position at the New School for Social Research in New York.

Three months earlier, the Oldens had placed their two-and-a-half-year-old daughter Maria Elisabeth (known as Kutzi) on a ship bound for Canada, for fear that she'd be interned by the British government or killed by a German bomb. As he'd said good-bye, he declared, "I shall never see her again!" Twenty-four hours after that emotional farewell, he was arrested and on his way, after the obligatory couple of interim stops, to the Isle of Man. Newly released, he and Ika had booked passage on the *City of Benares* in order to collect their daughter in Canada before heading to his new position and their new life in Manhattan.

The couple survived the initial impact blast, but as the rush to get to the lifeboats began, Rudolf Olden realized he had a serious problem. He was so sick and infirm that he knew he would face a real struggle to make it to the top deck of a ship fast taking on water, already starting to list.

As alarm bells rang and the corridors filled with smoke, panic was in the air. . . .

On January 30, 1933, President Paul von Hindenburg named Adolf Hitler, leader of the National Socialist German Workers' Party, the chancellor of Germany. Within days, his government had imposed restrictions on "personal liberty, on the right of free expression of opinion, including freedom of the press, on the right of assembly and the right of association." The Nazis also introduced the government's right to eavesdrop on telephone calls, to search houses, and to confiscate property.

As one of the Nazis' most vocal opponents, Rudolf Olden immediately got involved in a liberal effort to establish a congress in Berlin where those opposing Hitler's attempts to curb media freedoms could come together and speak out against the new regime. The venue for Das Freie Wort (The Free Word) was the Kroll Opera House, where 1,500 artists, writers, scientists, and left-leaning politicians gathered at short notice to voice their dismay at where the nation seemed to be heading.

It's a measure of his standing in the country at the time that Olden was named head of the congress. He also delivered one of the keynote addresses, a stirring call to arms about the freedoms of the press that were now under grave threat. As if to hammer home the tightening grip Hitler had on the country, police eventually rushed the stage and announced that the meeting was over, ironically enough, just as Wolfgang Heine, a Social Democrat politician, began speaking about "Freedom of Assembly."

Chaos briefly ensued, but after first defiantly belting out the socialist standard, "The Internationale" and the German labor anthem *"Brüder, zur Sonne, zur Freiheit"* (Brothers, to the Sun, to Freedom), the delegates eventually dispersed.

"Many certainly had the feeling, as did I," wrote Count Harry Kessler, delegate, writer, and diplomat, "that this would be the last time in Berlin where intellectuals could publicly stand up for freedom."

That Olden stood up to be counted at this final gathering of those who believed in and espoused liberty in Germany was inevitable. Much of his professional career had been spent in the service of liberal causes, battling injustice on different fronts, and striving to tamp down right-wing extremists who had long threatened the stability of the country and human rights therein.

Olden was born on January 14, 1885, in Stettin, then German territory in what is now Poland. Olden's mother was Rosa Stein, and his father, Johann August Oppenheim. Both were actors, and Johann also wrote under the pseudonym Hans Olden, eventually legally taking that as his name. Although Hans deserted the family, his son, originally Gunther, opted to change his name to Rudolf Olden in 1915, the first name paying homage to an uncle, Prince Rudolf of Liechtenstein, at whose home he had spent much of his childhood.

Keeping that sort of illustrious company in his formative years had an inevitable impact. As a young man, Olden was conservative and far removed from the future left-wing firebrand he would become, scourge of the Nazis and Hitler.

"Rudi," wrote his brother Balder, "who later counted any day without a battle as a day wasted, was at the age of fifteen, the complete gentleman. No speck of dust was to be found on his always perfectly pressed suit; his immaculate manners could become decidedly frosty: he was slim, tall, aristocratic in every gesture."

That description is borne out by his membership in a dueling society at school, a hobby that left him with lifelong scars. At the outbreak of World War I, he enlisted with the Darmstadt Dragoons, twice being injured during active service in Belgium and on the Eastern Front. Having passed the bar just before the conflict began, he saw out the remainder of the war working in the court-martials department of the army. Though so often later identified with pacifism, he spoke fondly of his military service, even if it always came tinged with disdain for the Junker officer class (the upper class/nobles who made up the officers in the army).

He married Ika in Vienna in 1920 and began a journalism career that was not without controversy. With his friend Hugo Bettauer, he briefly co-published *Er und Sie. Wochenschrift für Lebenskultur und Erotik* ("He and She. Weekly Paper for Lifestyle and Eroticism"), a daring and progressive venture that campaigned for women's and gay rights. It also brought a failed attempt to indict the pair for indecency, and his partner was eventually assassinated by a member of the National Socialist Party in 1925.

While in Austria, Olden also wrote for *Der Friede*, and *Der Neue Tag*, liberal publications, before moving to Berlin to take up the position of political editor with the *Berliner Tageblatt*, the preeminent liberal newspaper of the Weimar era.

Concomitantly, he had been licensed at the German Supreme Court in 1924 and soon gained a reputation as a human rights lawyer. Among his more celebrated victories was securing a posthumous pardon for Josef Jakubowsky, a former Russian soldier who in 1926 was wrongfully convicted of murdering a three-year-old boy in Mecklenburg. He also defended Carl Ossietzky, on trial for exposing Germany's breaches of the military restrictions imposed by the Treaty of Versailles.

His most direct intersection with the emerging force that was Hitler came in 1931 when Hans Litten, a lawyer who some regarded as Olden's protégé, called the leader of the Nazis to the witness stand in the Eden Dance Palace Trial. In a case where four brown-shirted storm troopers faced charges of assault and attempted murder, Litten spent three hours quizzing Hitler about whether or not his movement believed that they should gain power by violent means if they could not do so via politics. Writing in the *Berliner Tageblatt* the next morning, Olden pointed out that by forcing the future Führer to swear he would obey the constitution, Litten was hoping to lose Hitler some of his more hard-core supporters.

"Hitler swears and swears to his legality," wrote Olden, ominously. "[F]ew believe him."

As his career ran along twin tracks, with space in between for membership in a body like the German League for Human Rights and authoring a book on Gustav Stresemann in 1929, Olden was described by the writer Kurt Tucholsky as one of the two hundred figures who really counted for something in Berlin, an accolade that perhaps explains why he was so centrally involved with setting up and standing up for Das Freie Wort on February 19, 1933.

Just a week later, on the night of February 26, even as the Reichstag still burned, Olden received warning that the Nazis were arresting opponents of every political stripe, a notice designed to prompt him to flee. However, he opted to hang tough until the following morning because he was due in court as a defense lawyer and couldn't bear to let a client down. After discharging his legal duty, he discovered that his house was now under Gestapo surveillance, as was the Supreme Court, where he had an appointment later that day.

Olden decided discretion was the better part of valor. He never returned home, spending the night at a friend's house and plotting the quickest, safest way out of Germany.

He headed south the next morning, and when he reached the Zittau Mountains, pretended to be one more vacationing tourist. Clambering aboard a pair of wooden skis, he traveled cross-country on the snow, eventually slipping through the border with Czechoslovakia. An arduous trek for a forty-eight-year-old man, yet he knew as he skied through the wintry woods that his life, literally, depended on it.

All enemies of Hitler now had targets on their backs, and Olden had been a thorn in the side of the National Socialists and their leader as both journalist and lawyer since the mid-1920s. The need to get out fast was underscored by the fate of some of those he had fought for and worked alongside. Ossietzky and Litten were both arrested in the aftermath of the fire. The former died of tuberculosis after years spent in concentrations camps, and the latter committed suicide while being held at Dachau. The nightmare in Germany that Olden so often predicted in his writing was now coming true.

All of which explains why Olden hastened, like so many other writers and artists in a similar position, to the relative safety of Prague, where Ika—a psychotherapist, and daughter of the renowned Zionist economist, Georg Halpern—joined him the next day. Of course, the city was teeming with Germans on the run, and Olden soon hooked up with Wieland Herzfelde, whose career as a left-wing publisher in Weimar had also been ended by the rise of Hitler. Having been forced to flee the Gestapo, Herzfelde continued to operate his Malik imprint in exile, and in May of 1933, he published Olden's "*Hitler, der Erober. Die Entlarvung einer Legende*" ("Hitler the Conqueror: The Exposure of a Legend").

A bold pamphlet, it decried the myth of the Nazi leader by high-lighting the roles played by Paul von Hindenburg, Franz von Papen, and others in his unlikely ascent. Almost immediately banned in Germany, editions of it were published in Amsterdam and London as the decade wore on, and, as one of the first critical examinations of the Hitler phenomenon by an eyewitness, it would be widely quoted thereafter. It was also central to the Nazis finally revoking Olden's German citizenship on December 3, 1936, the same day a host of literary, trade union, and political figures, including Thomas Mann, suffered the same indignity.

Not long after the pamphlet first came out, Olden was on the move again, reaching Paris that summer via stops in Austria and Switzerland. During his brief sojourn in France, he received a commission from Comité des Délégations Juives and, with the assistance of Ika, he compiled *Das Schwarzbuch: Die lage der Juden in Deutschland 1933* (Black Book on the Situation of Jews in Germany, 1933: Facts and Documents). By the time that first major insight into the anti-Semitism then rife in his home country had been published, he had already crossed the channel to England.

In London, he helped to co-found the German PEN (Poets, Essayists, and Novelists) club in exile, a group of writers who had fled the Nazi regime and established their own unique chapter of the international literary organization. Aside from gaining worldwide recognition for so many prominent authors driven out of their homeland, it offered a support network, designed to assist them in staying one step ahead of the Nazis' ever increasing reach. To this end, Olden threw himself into the cause and, for the next seven years of his life, was indefatigable in his attempts to help those left behind.

"After the invasion of Austria by German troops in March, 1938," wrote Volkmar Zuhlsdorff in *Hitler's Exiles*, "Olden made particular efforts on behalf of Robert Musil, who was eventually brought to safety in Switzerland in August. Following the occupation of Czechoslovakia in March 1939, Olden worked with the Academy in Exile and the Arden Society to rescue those exiles who remained in Prague. The sheer number of appeals for help meant that he was on the verge of exhaustion, particularly as there were so many unexpected complications."

Olden came to the aid of others in the same way that individuals had tried to improve his own situation in England. In September 1935, Gilbert Murray, professor of Greek at the University of Oxford, gave him access to Yatscombe Cottage on the grounds of his house at Boar's Hill in the city. The following year, he began lecturing on "The Rise and Fall of German Liberalism" as a member of the faculty of social studies, and, on the back of that, was commissioned to write a book on the subject. On and off campus, he spoke repeatedly about the existential threat the Nazis posed, not just to his home country, but to England, too.

He supplemented his burgeoning academic career with freelance journalism, writing articles about England for *Das Argentinische Tageblatt*, a German-language publication in Buenos Aires with a determinedly anti-Nazi editorial stance. Even though he had found meaningful work and a thriving intellectual environment in Oxford, Olden did not forget those who had not been as fortunate to escape when he did. He did his best to promote the causes of Ossietzky and Litten, in particular, using his influence with English lawyers to try to secure the release of both men.

"He played a very active role, along with other refugees, in campaigning for ex-colleagues and friends who had not escaped, but were in prison, concentration camps or otherwise detained in Germany," wrote Charmian Brinson and Marian Malet in *Ark of Civilization*. "The method used by the refugees was to work through sympathetic persons of influence in their countries of refuge, to inform them of events in Germany and get more news into the newspapers so that pressure could be put on foreign governments to oppose the Nazis."

Whether addressing the PEN international congress in Edinburgh or lecturing about "Germany and the Jews" to the Oxford University Jewish Society at Somerville College, Olden seemed driven by a desire to be a voice for the voiceless and to offer an eyewitness's crucial insight into what Hitler was trying to achieve.

"Rudolf Olden was one of the most outstanding personalities of the German emigration. With all his many-sided and varied gifts, he knew of only one goal towards which he worked untiringly: to fight for a free and freed Germany," wrote his friend and fellow Hutchinson internee Friedrich Burschell. "He threw the weight of his whole personality into the service for this idea; his friends know how unsparingly he used himself up in the midst of all the difficulties and obstacles that blocked his path. But he was tough—he never gave in. In earlier days, he had, as editor of the *Berliner Tageblatt*, fought against German militarism and imperialism; he later identified his cause with the cause of Ossietzky's and all those many others persecuted on political grounds. Since 1935, he struggled in the same way with all the difficult problems of the emigration."

A somewhat regular contributor to the letters page of *The Guardian*, Olden co-authored a missive in August 1939, with war clouds gathering, listing all the Austrian and German writers in exile implacably opposed to the Nazi government. Later that year, he wrote an opinion column for the newspaper entitled, "What Is Going to Become of Germany?" in which he explored the possibility of a military dictatorship wresting control back from Hitler.

By the time that article appeared, the Home Office had categorized him as an "Enemy Alien," and the description bristled. Everything he had said or written (at that point he was working on a book called *Is Germany a Hopeless Case?*) since fleeing Berlin had been critical of Hitler and his cronies, and designed to inform the wider world of the true nature of the menace he posed. This was a drum he'd been beating years before the rest of the world learned the rhythm.

"I deeply feel I did not deserve this," wrote Olden to a friend.

Of course, things were only going to get worse. On June 25, 1940, twenty-four hours after he and Ika had placed their darling daughter Kutzi on a ship to Canada, he was arrested and interned, first at Southampton and then at Warth Mills, before finally being ferried to the Isle of Man and Hutchinson Camp. Two days after his internment, *The Guardian* published a letter he'd sent to them before the authorities came calling. In it, he questioned the wisdom of the internment mania sweeping Britain.

"By calling them 'enemy aliens,' putting them under humiliation, restrictions, dismissing them from their posts, hunting them out of their living places . . . ?" he asked. "Is this the preparation for future alliance with them? Had these potential revolutionaries come to this country to learn that only 'blood' matters? To learn that it is a British rule that every-one who takes a stand against his own government is untrustworthy, that he must be treated like an outlaw? To learn that to fight for principles is shameful and dishonorable?"

Olden's physical condition when he disembarked in Douglas was not good. Still, when he was invited to give lectures on political affairs, sometimes three hundred inmates would gather on the lawn outside to listen to him speak. Even in fine, warm weather, he delivered his talks with an overcoat pulled tight around his frame, and those sitting near the front could see him nervously rolling a single blade of grass between his fingers. He had no need to worry. The audience was rapt at his analysis of the contemporary geopolitical situation and his ability to invoke literary references that spoke to their own plight.

"No one of us here will ever forget those summer days when Olden would sit with us on the lawn," wrote Heinrich Fraenkel, "his clear blue eyes looking across the barbed wire, out to the sea: then he would talk to us of *Michael Kohlhaas*, [von] Kleist's immortal story of the man who hated injustice so much that he went berserk in his desperate urge to right a wrong that had been done to him. Not one of us but was touched to the core by that story's deep significance for ourselves—not our present little inconvenience, but the big task in which we once had, and hoped to have again, a share."

Even as he played a full part in the cultural and intellectual life of the camp, others had taken up the cudgel on his behalf. At Oxford, Professor Murray was on the case.

"There are many other refugees in the University whose release from internment is desirable," he wrote to the Oxford vice-chancellor. "But I doubt if there is anyone who has so devoted himself to the struggle against Hitlerism as his main interest in life."

This point was being made on the other side of the Atlantic Ocean, too. Prince Hubertus zu Löwenstein, whom Olden had given his first gig as a journalist, went to the British Embassy in Washington to plead that Olden's was a very special case. There, he had an encounter with an official whose intransigence captured the madness of the time.

"Any German in England ought to be locked up in a concentration camp!" said Mr. A. C. E. Malcolm.

"Look here!" said zu Löwenstein. "While Olden and others who you have now interned were fighting Hitler, you were still flirting with him!"

Much closer to home, the same point was made in a more elongated way in the House of Commons.

"I understand that a very famous author who has long written books against Hitler and has been struggling against Hitler, for many years, has been put into an internment camp," said George Strauss, a Labour MP for Lambeth North, in a speech on July 10. "He is Rudolf Olden, and he wrote a book called *Hitler, the Pawn*, as well as other books. His position cannot be in doubt. Now, he can no longer carry on his anti-Nazi propaganda. . . . These are Category C people. There is no suspicion about the Category C people, and I do not think there can be. What is the public purpose or common sense in putting that kind of person into an internment camp?"

Two weeks after Strauss spoke out, Ivor C. Lewis of the Progressive League in London wrote to *The Guardian* about the ludicrous policy of interning the enemies of Hitler, and cited examples of anti-fascist fighters like Olden. While all these various entreaties were being made, the man himself settled down and made quite the impact on his surroundings.

"To be interned with Rudolf Olden was similar to being interned with James Cameron [a celebrated and prolific English writer, war correspondent, and broadcaster]," said Klaus Hinrichsen, in a reference to the varied, fascinating career he'd had and the polyglot character he was. "Somebody who has been everywhere, somebody who has interviewed all the great politicians and has a world-wide view and philosophic approach to everything."

Olden's stay at Hutchinson was just three weeks long, yet his contribution in that time to camp life, in many ways, helped to set the tone for what was to come, in particular the manner in which so many internees sought to maximize their time in captivity thereafter. Despite the negative impact on his own mental and physical health, he put himself front and center in the crucial opening weeks, contributing greatly to the intellectual mood being forged.

He was released on August 8, 1940, but only on the condition that he book immediate passage out of England. It was as if he was perceived to be some sort of threat to the war effort, not an anti-Hitler activist whose well-being had been severely compromised by his internment on top of so many years in peripatetic exile from his homeland.

"That broke his faith," said his brother Peter of Olden's time behind barbed wire. "He became a sick and despairing man."

Contemporary newspaper reports described him as being confined to his room upon release, nearly unable to move, a diagnosis confirmed in a despairing letter Olden wrote to Friedrich Burschell in the weeks after leaving Hutchinson, while awaiting his departure from Liverpool.

"I am in the grip of a profound disinclination for life," Olden wrote. "The doctors cannot identify any illness and call it a nervous breakdown. I sense the cause of my illness; it is revulsion, at anything and everything, physical and mental, and it seems hard to convince oneself that the extraordinary effort required to overcome the revulsion could ever be duly rewarded again."

On the day he boarded the *City of Benares* at Liverpool, as if to confirm his persona non grata status in Britain, his passport was marked "No permission to return."

What happened in the moments after the torpedo struck the ship in the Atlantic Ocean is inevitably attended by confusion and various versions of events. But, even in the mayhem that ensued in the thirty minutes between the moment of impact and the ship sinking, there were no reports of Rudolf Olden ever making it to the top deck, the only chance of being saved. Ika was finally persuaded—she was reluctant, as her husband was still below—to clamber into Lifeboat 6 by Colonel James Baldwin-Webb, a Conservative Party MP for The Wrekin, in Shropshire, who performed heroically that night before going down with the ship.

Half the people in Lifeboat 6 fell out as it was lowered into the water at too steep an angle. Rudolf and Ika were among the 298 souls, including 77 children, who died on the *Benares* that night.

When reports began to filter around the world that the Nazis had killed so many innocents, their propaganda arm swung into action, immediately alleging that Olden and Baldwin-Webb (on a Red Cross mission to Canada) were on a clandestine joint operation to Washington with the intent of persuading the United States government to join the war on the British side.

Around Hutchinson Square, news of Olden's death arrived six days later. The cloud it cast over the camp was one more measure of the impact he had had there in such a short time. To the men who had been lucky enough to wander into his orbit during that sojourn, his loss was deemed "irreparable."

"In Rudolf Olden, we not only loose [sic] the historian, as rich in knowledge and ideas, not only the fascinating speaker and the courageous defender of the Cause of Justice," wrote Burschell in *The Camp* newspaper. "We also loose [sic] a self-sacrificing friend, one of our best comrades, a chivalrous, generous and charming man, an outstanding representative of that 'Better Germany' in which he himself so fervently believed. His last letters to me were about our camp here, and his last greetings were for his friends for whom he wanted to continue working. We owe it to his immortal memory to try to follow his example."

It is an illustration of his standing outside of Hutchinson that his death reverberated around the globe. Heinrich Breunig, last chancellor of the Weimar Republic, was by then the Lucius N. Littauer Professor of Government at Harvard University. When he read about the sinking of the *Benares*, he stated that Olden's death was "the heaviest blow which post-war German politics could have suffered." In *The Guardian*, a Hungarian newspaper owner also exiled in England, wrote a tribute.

"Shall I say that this period of captivity shook his faith in his mission?" asked Baron Louis Hatvany. "Even after his release he did not, it seems, recover confidence in himself, so badly had it been undermined by the humiliation that his release was not granted on account of his beliefs but because he had received a call to an American university. Up to the last moment, he hoped against hope that this country, which he had grown to feel as his own, would find some use for him. I remember seeing him wave a newspaper cutting that Mr. Duff Cooper would be glad to avail himself of the services of well-known anti-Nazis once they were set free. 'The papers have reported that I am free: I am waiting, waiting, but nobody has sent for me!'"

That view was corroborated by Storm Jameson, president of London PEN, who was close to both Rudolf and Ika. She wrote a paean to the pair in which she noted Rudolf's reluctance to leave and his crushing disappointment at the authorities' failure to realize that he, somebody who had been calling out Hitler long before his true menace became obvious to others, could be of genuine use in the fight against the Nazis. The latter point was emphasized in another piece by a fellow internee from Hutchinson.

"Of the men who have been with us in this camp, the finest is no more," wrote Heinrich Fraenkel. "He was given leave to go to America, and the ship was torpedoed. The Nazis got him after all. They had been trying hard enough these seven years."

CHAPTER SIX

All the News That's Fit to Print

*The Camp Fathers, supported by the kindness of the Commander, wel-
come the birth and first appearance of our Camp Journal very heart-
ily. Taking in[to] account existing circumstances, a Journal like this
must of necessity be limited in its scope, but in spite of this, we con-
fidently hope it will be worthwhile having. Our chief endeavor will
be to further the feeling and the spirit of fellowship. The Journal will
mirror in a serious as well as humorous vein, our difficult situation.*
                                    —THE CAMP, SEPTEMBER 21, 1940

ON THE COVER OF THE THIRD ISSUE OF *THE CAMP* NEWSPAPER ON
October 6, Michael Corvin, its first editor, wrote a rather stern piece
under the headline "Realism." Among other topics, he called on internees
to appreciate that, when it came to agitating for mass releases, a lot was
being done, inside and outside the square, on their behalf. The fledgling
publication had received many complaints about the glacial pace of the
process as their applications wended their way through the labyrinthine
British bureaucracy. Corvin wanted readers to realize that they weren't
living in a dictatorship anymore and, in a functioning democracy, these
sorts of decisions took more time.

He reminded the internees that "important newspapers like the
Manchester Guardian" were fighting for their cause, and that the authorities at Hutchinson had been generous to the men at all times. Against
that slightly obsequious background, he demanded more perspective and

less criticism of those in charge, since those individuals had very little to do with issuing release orders.

"Nobody denies that our situation is a difficult one," wrote Corvin. "But just because that is so, just because we feel tried and tired and tested—we should remember the reason which causes this hardship. . . . The majority of us have now been interned for about three months, during which time the war [has] developed into a more terrible state than ever before. We are keen to do our bit for the victory of justice and freedom. We may be sure not to be forgotten or overlooked. We are fully entitled to hope for ourselves in a near future. For the time being, we are serving the cause, which we are fighting for best by keeping steady and looking forward without becoming impatient."

While many around the square were angered by the editorial, this plea for patience was the cry of a man who had already been through quite a lot himself. Michael Corvin was the pen name of Leo Freund, a journalist who, even by the standards of so many remarkable internees, boasted quite the biography. Before Hitler took power, he had worked for the *Berliner Tageblatt*, a liberal newspaper, and had lived in a fashionable apartment on Hohenzollerndamm with his wife Yadya, his son Assar, and a German shepherd called Prince. Then, the Nazis gained control and he and his family were soon on the run.

"I am a refugee from Nazi oppression and was classified as such by the Aliens Tribunal, Clerkenwell Police Court, London, on October 13, 1939," wrote Corvin. "Technically it might be argued that I didn't enter Britain as a refugee, as I came to her not directly from Germany. However, I left Germany finally in Spring 1935, as a fugitive from the Gestapo for reasons of race and journalist activities. If I had been unable to evade Nazi laws, my fate would have been no different to that of tens of thousands of Jews and anti-Nazis."

The family's escape took them south to Spain before moving to England where he garnered work as a correspondent for the *Neue Freie Presse* (Vienna) in their London office—at least until Hitler's stranglehold on the Austrian press meant even overseas Jewish freelancers were no longer going to be employed. Interned on December 6, 1939, long before Churchill's "Collar the lot!" paranoia about fifth columnists, Corvin was placed aboard the SS *Arandora Star*, a cruise ship pressed into service as a transport vessel and tasked with carrying 1,200 Italian and German internees to Canada.

The *Arandora Star* left Liverpool on July 1, 1940, and was sunk by a single torpedo from a German U-boat off the northwest coast of Ireland the following day. The ship went down in just half an hour, killing 734 Italians (many of whom had been happily living in Scotland for years before the war broke out) and 175 Germans. Survivors, including Corvin, were taken back to Britain, where Corvin ended up spending the duration of the war at various Isle of Man camps. Hutchinson was his first stop, and through the medium of *The Camp*, the one where he had the most enduring impact.

The first issue of the newspaper was published on September 21, 1940, using an old Gestetner duplicating machine initially supplied to the internees by Commander Daniel in order to print flyers and informational leaflets. That Daniel recognized how a regular publication about life around Hutchinson Square might also contribute positively to their environment is obvious given the main article on page one, "Commander's Introduction," in which he acknowledged the special character of the internees.

"The publication of a Camp Journal comes in the natural sequences of new enterprises which, I am glad to say, happen with great regularity in Hutchinson Camp," wrote Daniel. "It is a matter of congratulation that men of all classes, brought together under present conditions, have been able so quickly to acclimatize and organize themselves."

While he also used the space to advertise forthcoming attractions, such as a purpose-built hall and showers, and to ask for patience regarding the release process, it was the Camp Fathers in their own introduction, featured down the front page, who set out a mission statement for what the newspaper might be.

"It will be a focus of our cultural efforts, it will deal with our concerns about destitute question [*sic*], and with all these manifold and varied problems and projects that have one aim only—to ease our lot, to make it more bearable and to help one another," they wrote. "There is, however, one thing that our Journal must and will show in these difficult times with quiet clarity, and that is our unshakeable confidence in the final triumph of Justice and Liberty."

If that screed sounds like they were hopeful *The Camp* could be all things to all people at Hutchinson, the publication faced an immediate and important debate about its identity before the first pages were even run through the duplicator. A letter to the editor that predated publication and made it into the debut issue asked a pertinent question about language.

Dear Editor,

Most of us appreciate the idea to publish a weekly newspaper but we are anxious to inform you of some perhaps important wishes. First of all: There are many colleagues in this camp whose knowledge of English is rather limited. For them a newspaper in German would be more adequate. Should that be impossible, perhaps a few items could be printed in the German language. In a certain connection with this, one is another proposal: Could you possibly fix on the notice board besides the Isle of Man Times each afternoon, a very brief "News-Extract," translated in German? I am sure that would be a welcome help for a lot of us.

Truly yours
R. P.

Choosing what language to speak, never mind to print, was a significant issue from the first day. Obviously, all Germans and Austrians spoke German, but there was a marked reluctance from many to continue to converse in their mother tongue. Even if some had only pidgin English, there was a widespread belief that, since these refugees from the Nazis wanted to be considered prospective British citizens, they should always be heard speaking that language, regardless of how limited their grasp of it. Others thought this wholly impractical, especially those who one day aspired to return to their homelands once Hitler had been defeated. Ultimately, the majority of the internees compromised and spoke a hybrid of the two tongues.

All notices from the authorities were printed only in English, and all announcements over the public address system were in English, as well. In the interest of promoting and reinforcing the idea to skeptical outsiders that Hutchinson contained men who had renounced Hitler and the Germany he had fashioned, *The Camp* was written predominantly in English, with occasional pieces in German or Yiddish.

The language debate was only part of what would become the newspaper's ongoing identity crisis. While every periodical goes through stages of discovering its true purpose, especially one born under duress, this publication was under particular scrutiny from the start.

The questions were myriad. Was its function to entertain the internees? Was it somehow supposed to show the outside world the caliber of people being held there? Was it a forum through which they could campaign for release? Perhaps, at its best, it was an amalgam of all of the above. Certainly, the nature of its precise role was debated around the square, where many were less impressed by the achievement in producing a paper than they were annoyed at its failure to impact directly on their personal situations. Which, to be fair, it was never going to be able to do.

Editorially, the first issue was, as might be expected, a bit of a mixed bag. Aside from the introductions, there was a piece mocking the new shower baths, an account of recent musical performances, and a review of the camp's first art exhibition. The opening of a Technical School was praised in a puff piece, and announcements were made about the arrival of a Torah in the square and the advent of a Youth Group, established to cater to the needs and interests of the teenagers in the population. Additional features included a Letters to the Editor section, a wordplay quiz, an essay calling for the introduction of sport to the daily routine, and Friedrich Burschell's moving requiem for Rudolf Olden.

That the paper was embattled from the beginning is obvious from subsequent issues. The first page of the second issue, published on September 29, was given over to a lengthy, unsigned defense of the already beleaguered publication. In it, the writer asks the critics to appreciate the obstacles that had to be negotiated in order to bring the thing into existence and then implores them, especially those who were uniquely qualified, to assist those involved if they wanted it to be better.

"We were fully aware of the fact that the start—with difficulties unknown to the readers and probably underestimated by them—was not and could not be a startling success. But we hope, on the other hand, that after this much criticized beginning, some of the many gifted writers, journalists and men of all professions find their way in our lofty emporium to help us and the camp in having a newspaper of real value."

The writer ended the editorial with a reminder of the bizarre conditions under which it was being produced: "We are not a free newspaper in the sense of the law, but thanks to the commander we are free in the moral sense, and thus able to give a constructive criticism of whatever disturbs us. We, therefore, appeal to you, reader, for this kind of creative criticism in this paper which belongs to you and wishes to represent you."

Just beneath the article was a box advertising the intention to put a mailbox for Letters to the Editor outside *The Camp* office. In a change from initial policy, the editorial staff also requested authors of any future missives to attach their full name to their work. A reasonable enough proviso; however, the call for increased dialogue and assistance must not have gone down too well, given that Corvin had to deliver his clarion call for "Realism" in the very next issue.

Much as internees quibbled about the fact that the paper wasn't doing enough to press for their release, Corvin presided over a publication willing to fight their corner on certain issues. After pleading for them to be more realistic about their situation and the paper's role in improving it in the third issue, he devoted the front page of the fourth issue, published just nine days later, to "An Open Letter to the Commander," demanding meaningful employment for internees.

After serious consideration and after a long discussion with Mr. Hughes of the Society of Friends, the responsible leaders of Hutchinson Camp regard it as their duty to put before you the question of work for this Camp. The reason is not only [because] the number of destitutes rises from week to week and that the purchasing power of the internees goes down accordingly. This fills us with great anxiety, and we know that you share our feelings.

That, however, is not all. We believe that the internees should obtain a chance to make full use of their time, which is now being wasted. We do not want Red Cross or any other Prisoner of War work. We want to prove our loyalty to Great Britain and our hatred of Nazism, and it is our aim to participate to the best of our ability in the industrial War effort of this country. . . . Will you please help us by allowing us to help the country?

Some of the editorial decisions show that Corvin and his cohorts were keenly aware that they were, rightly or wrongly, considered the collective voice of the men. Yet the paper never spared its readers from criticism. On the very next page of the issue that contained the open letter, there was a feisty article attacking malingerers, beneath the capitalized headline, "THESE LINES CONCERN YOU—YOU PERSONALLY."

You do not like our Camp paper, you want a different sort of writing, very strong, very radical, fighting all and everything, fighting the Commander, fighting the Home Office, fighting against internment. You want to be released. You think that it is wrong they interned you. You are perfectly right and we fully agree. We too want to fight, and, believe it or not, we shall fight. Only our ways are different: we do not fight by means of helpless and hopeless discussions, by attacking authorities who might help us, by grumbling and complaining. OUR weapons are facts, facts which will prove that we are not enemy aliens but friends and helpers of this country. That there is only one faith in a happy future and one hatred against the common enemy. YOU MUST HELP US, YOU PERSONALLY! WHAT DO YOU WANT US TO DO?

There followed an outline of how the grumblers needed to stop moaning and to get busy trying to help. In a lengthy diatribe that also featured a summation of the recent geopolitical history that had brought them all to this particular place, the unnamed author implored malcontents to lend their weight to changing the situation by contributing to the greater good, whether it be by teaching a class, taking a class, or even writing an article about their own story.

As editor, Corvin was conscious of how put-upon the residents felt. When the *Isle of Man Times* impugned the reputation of the men by calling them "Huns," Corvin commissioned Heinrich Fraenkel to pen a feisty response on behalf of a community disgusted at being regarded by anybody as in any way pro-Hitler. Then he ensured that there were plenty of other elements of the paper designed to send that same message. Cartoons were a regular medium for making those—and other—political points.

Here's Hitler dressed as a pretty girl in a meadow, replete with bonnet, pulling the petals off a flower as he tries to decide whether or not to invade Britain. There's an illustration of his tombstone with the gag, "This is definitely my last territorial demand." Not all attempts at humor were so overtly political. A drawing of two showgirls chatting contained the speech bubble, "My boyfriend is a conscientious objector. Poor thing! What does he do instead?"

That and a whole host of other illustrations in the first six issues came from the artist known as ESTE, the pen name of Eric (Ernst) Stern, a renowned stage designer from Berlin. His contributions to *The Camp* ran the gamut. Some were full-page efforts, such as his farewell piece featuring Stern in a British army uniform flanked by women as he declares, "I'm joining up and going to see some real girls!" Others were tiny graphics at the bottom of a page, like one sketch that details a turtle carrying a bag marked "Internees' Mail," a caustic commentary on how long letters took to reach the men.

His work was often nakedly political and brilliantly conceived. One image shows a gentleman pianist in a frock coat giving a classical concert in which he's reading the musical notes from sheet music that runs along the barbed wire around the square—as cogent a commentary on their circumstances at Hutchinson as anything. Stern's impact was such that upon his departure, Corvin and Wilhelm Feuchtwang, the newspaper administrator, wrote a joint paean to him, and weeks after he'd gone, they ran a caption competition where readers could come up with a punchline to accompany ESTE's drawing of two internees carrying a trash can full of herring back to their kitchen, a morning ritual in every house.

"Saturday last, our dear friend and collaborator ESTE, Eric [Ernst] Stern, left Hutchinson Camp to join the AMPC [Auxiliary Military Pioneer Corps]. We are sure to express not only our regrets but those of many readers to lose a contributor whose cartoons brightened the paper so brilliantly. On the other hand, we wish to congratulate him and wish him all the best. Good-bye, Eric, and good luck!"

There was a determined effort to inject humor into every issue. Witness Peter Blunder, a recurring character introduced in the third issue, the creation of somebody who signed his work DOL, and offered a very wry take on life within the camp. His opening gambit poked fun at the educated nature of the population, mocking the fact that there were so many residents with the "not quite Christian name of doctor." The commander was often in his sights, too, along with the Camp Father.

"There are 1,200 men in this dump of brain power and futility," wrote Blunder, who dropped the "h" to sound Cockney. "I was surprised to find only 879 different ideas 'ow to 'andle this blooming war. They agree on only one thing: that it might be difficult for old John Bull to destroy 'itler's power without their 'elp."

"DOL" was the nom de plume of Adolf Mirecki, a native of Ukraine and a product of the previous two turbulent decades in European history. Born in 1909 in Berdychiv, one of the most Jewish towns in the old Russian Empire, he ran away from home at thirteen, unhappy at his father's remarriage following his mother's death. The precocious teen walked nearly eight hundred miles to Vienna and there started to dabble in art, calling himself Adolf to blend in. By the 1930s, he was in Hamburg running a prosperous lumber business. At least, until fortune took a turn.

One of his customers decided to renege on a debt by reporting Mirecki's Jewishness to the Nazi authorities. Fortunately, Mirecki had enough friends in the port city to get smuggled out on a ship bound for England. At Hutchinson, he indulged his creative instincts via Blunder, an alter ego unafraid to call out fellow internees. For instance, he used the occasion of the camp's second art exhibition to write an article arguing for another exhibit to contain all the different characters around the square, the premise for him to hold forth on the amount of politicking and backbiting that went on around the place.

"It isn't this barbed wire which makes this lovely spot similar to a zoo," he wrote. "It's what they keep inside. Every reader of my enlightening stuff will agree with me that, besides 'imself, of course, there are a lot of strange birds in this cage. There would be, for example, the little mudslinger. The beast of usually less height than a normal grown-up man, is rather remarkable. It be'aves well, as long as you are standing before 'is eyes. But turn your back, and 'e begins business—'e slings mud and every kind of dirt with the 'elp of his enormously developed beak after you—a rare and not so pleasant phenomenon."

In another issue, Mirecki addressed the opportunity internees had to gain their freedom by enlisting in the AMPC, the branch of the military where refugees could serve, largely unarmed, as part of an army of unskilled handymen doing logistical and infrastructural work to support combat troops. Their prize for signing up was instant release—the Holy Grail.

To him, this was a no-brainer because, as he reminded his readers, "do you seriously believe in the next future, and until the monster is smitten, 'e will be free to do what 'e likes as in the old days of peace?" He also contributed regular cartoon strips mocking everything from the war effort and the indomitable British lion to the interminable release process and, of course, Hitler (depicted as a monkey on a branch eating his own tail).

As can be deduced from Blunder's work, *The Camp*'s wider editorial policy often reeked of "a spoonful of sugar helps the medicine go down." Even when it came to serious matters, there was a concerted effort to deliver the message with a smile. In the very first issue, a short piece about Air Raid Precautions (ARP) is equal parts comical and practical, starting out with an attempt to poke fun at the fact that "compoundians"—as it called the residents—were baffled at the change in ARP readiness rules. Then, going right into pragmatic advice, "Remember, if you hear short blasts of the whistle, make a beeline for your house, because fun and games are about to start. Should any of you gentlemen think of extinguishing an incendiary bomb by pouring a bucketful of water on it, you are reminded that this is the best way of going to heaven."

Feuchtwang, the administrator of the paper, was the son of the Chief Rabbi of Vienna, and had escaped the clutches of the Gestapo by fleeing to Rotterdam, where his sister was married to the Chief Rabbi of that city—the background of the man who ensured that the early issues of *The Camp* featured lots of practical notices about religious matters. After Rabbi Dr. Holzer wrote briefly in English about the delight at the arrival of a Torah, he contributed another article in German in the second issue, where two pages were given over to coverage of the Jewish New Year and other matters pertaining to the religion. These included a calendar of notable days in the Hebrew Year 5701 and an un-bylined explanation of the role of the Jewish Cultural Center that also served as a rallying cry.

"Everyone who belongs to the Jewish people, feels the urgency—just in our time and position—to reexamine his inner situation with a view to develop and deepen his knowledge of what it means to him to be a Jew. There lies a unique chance for every one of us to form this depressing time of internment to a time which brings into renewed existence internal strength of our Jewish soul. We must help each other in that grand but difficult task in the atmosphere and spirit of real comradeship. That is the aim and programme of the Jewish Cultural Center, to be a rallying point, a central platform comprising everyone who belongs to the Jewish people to be a stimulus for Jewish Cultural life in our Camp."

It succeeded in that regard. Ulli Hirsch, a hugely influential economist—formerly price control administrator in World War I Germany, and later, state secretary for economics in the Weimar Republic—wrote an evocative essay about the thriving Jewish community in the square, the impact of the rabbis, and the way in which the men came together to somehow build sukkah huts (traditional Jewish structures constructed during the festival of Sukkot) in October of 1940:

When I remember the solemn services and the inspiring speeches our Rabbis held, specially on the high festivals with the holy quietness spread all over the camp . . . when I remember the joy of the tabernacles with the small, unsteady and shabby huts we built with nearly no material but great zeal and enthusiasm, which we decorated inside as if they were destined for kings and princes. When we were sitting in those huts we did not even feel the chilly air when singing, learning and rejoicing the joy of our festival.

And it is not merely a formal act when we keep our religious rites with all their symbols, although not appreciated or understood by many. In spite of all difficulties and hindrances, their eternal values and meanings become more disclosed to those who are going deeper into our religious love, which are essential elements for forming and shaping a life devoted to self-discipline, righteousness and justice based on real love to God and man.

When I remember the weekly celebration of our Oneg Shabbat, which really makes us forget all outside events for some hours, or when I remember the manifold Jewish cultural activities, the many hours daily and nightly spent studying and learning our ancient history and literature, our Talmud with its immense spiritual wealth, which produces a better world before our eyes—then we are doing more than others who mourn, run around in resentment and bewail their fate.

Like any newspaper, *The Camp* was a notice board and a community focal point, one minute advertising how many men wanted more sport and culture, the next, running satirical columns poking fun at inefficiencies in the post office and the canteen. As unhappy as many readers were at its perceived lack of interest in campaigning for their release, there is no doubt the publication carried some weight in the commander's office. Within four weeks of the open letter demanding meaningful employment for those who were interested, the ninth issue carried a first-person account from an internee who was, by then, working in a day-release scheme on local farms.

"Every morning before roll call some comrades meet at the gate, waiting, whether a farmer wants their hands," wrote a correspondent calling himself Emper. "What jobs are we doing? ... the picking of potatoes, sorting them, pulling out carrots, mangels [beets], and turnips, threshing, spreading out manure and the like. Sometimes the work is hard, but never too hard. Besides, there are some other reasons why I myself and quite a lot of my comrades like to do these jobs.

"Although guarded by sentries you feel very strange when leaving the barbed wire behind and something like liberty surrounding you. Standing on the field, looking at the hills, plains and forests around you, amidst all the beauty of the nature with a wide sky above you and the free soil beneath your feet, doing a useful job and so connected with the free people, you forget your sorrows—and feel yourself free."

The Camp lasted for fifteen months and published forty-four issues. Corvin was succeeded as editor by Henry Gustav Dittmar, whose résumé included a promising academic career under the celebrated German historian Veit Valentin and, bizarrely, in his last job before internment, a stint working for Harold Nicolson, then parliamentary under-secretary for information. Others to assume the mantle thereafter included the German writer Freimut Schwarz, the graphic artist Carlo Pietzner, and Hans Schulze, who had edited *The Onchan Pioneer* during his time at another of the island's camps.

Harry P. Cemach was a one-off contributor to *The Camp*. After three months at Hutchinson, he was released in October 1940 to join the AMPC, where he spent two years building camps for British and American troops before eventually transferring to the Royal Army Ordnance Corps, and rising to the rank of captain. Two weeks after sailing out of Douglas for the last time, Cemach wrote a piece for the eighth issue under the headline "We're in the Army Now!" that he gleefully signed "Private H. Cemach."

"For us, who have been in uniform a fortnight now, it seems strange that we were in a place where there are 'releases' and where it was an achievement to be able to listen to the wireless," wrote Cemach, elaborating on a reunion of several Hutchinson alumni in his barracks. "We have become new men in a bare fortnight. New men, and free men! If any of us came here to be more comfortable I suppose they were disappointed. A soldier's life has no room for the many niceties of Hutchinson life, which I now begin to appreciate. Roll call here is a different matter, and if you are not very well shaven you are in for a bad time. No hiding in the third rank here."

Cemach then issued a call to arms, reminding his former colleagues that upon departure on a wet October morning he'd urged the remaining internees to "Come with us!" Now, he wanted to change that slightly, asking them to "Come to us!" For him, the task of defeating Germany was a job for "Men from Hutchinson." Cemach was perhaps more invested than most in having his fellow refugees lend their weight to the British cause, as upon release he had also written a vehement letter to the *Isle of Man Times*.

Like Heinrich Fraenkel, he had been greatly offended by the island's newspaper describing the internees as "Huns," so, under the name HC, he sent an angry denunciation to the editor of the *Isle of Man Times*, wanting to educate the journalists involved and their readers about the true nature of the men of Hutchinson Camp. Making the case that the residents of the square were the victims of wrongful imprisonment, he pointed out that they were not enemy spies, definitely not Nazis, and, in every case he knew of, great friends of Britain. The paper ran the piece under the headline "An Ex-internee Attacks the *Times*," while posting a reply defending their position and the policy of internment.

A sequel to this particular interaction would have to wait until the war was over.

CHAPTER SEVEN

Call Me by My Name

It is a story which redounds to the credit of many figures of British public life and of many ordinary British men and women; to the shame of others. A story of muddle and malfaisance; a story which shows how the ordinary refugees profited or suffered from their enforced isolation, often both at the same time; a story which brought out the best in some and the worst in others; a story which has its brutal as well as its bizarre elements, its humour as well as its tragedy. A story which is worth recalling.
—RONALD STENT, *A BESPATTERED PAGE*, 1980

RONALD STENT WAS PUT IN CHARGE OF THE CANTEEN AT HUTCHINSON. That he had some experience working in the kitchens of previous camps no doubt helped his candidacy, but not as much as the fact that his best friend Fritz Hallgarten had been appointed welfare officer and held some sway. It was a prestigious role that entitled Stent to certain privileges, as well as responsibilities. It was up to him to keep the place stocked with goods that the internees could purchase with whatever cash they had brought with them or managed to earn. To this end, his greatest perk of all was a weekly trip down the hill into Douglas.

Under armed guard, and much to the envy of his fellow prisoners, he walked through the gates and set off to stock up on whatever cigarettes and chocolate he could find to buy—not easy commodities to pick up once war rationing had kicked in. Even under the most strained circumstances the residents of Hutchinson didn't cut him much slack regarding the way he ran the canteen. Indeed, one of them wrote a letter to *The Camp* newspaper, advising him to "take a thick broom and work like a charwoman. There is much rubbish in the corners."

Still, for a man living behind barbed wire, it was worth enduring criticism because the simple act of grocery shopping offered him relief from his mundane existence.

"The barbed wire, the very symbol of all we were fighting against, became an obsession, an *idée fixe*, which made it impossible for a lot of irredeemably individualistic people to submit to the common weal," wrote Stent. "No doubt that was the reaction of many internees, particularly the older ones, but it was by no means universal."

Stent's job presented an opportunity to leave behind the square for a couple of hours, to meander along the streets of the Manx capital, and to stroll through Woolworths on Strand Street, browsing the shelves, rubbing shoulders with customers, almost like a free man. Four months into his internment, Stent was presented with an opportunity to become just that once again when recruitment began for the alien companies of the AMPC.

In July of 1940, the British government had produced a White Paper, revised and updated in August, outlining eighteen different categories of internees eligible for immediate release from the camps, and detailing the application process. Among the demographics deemed to no longer need confinement were boys under sixteen, men over seventy, invalids, ministers of religion, and the infirm. Others reckoned to be eligible were those who held a work permit issued by the Alien War Service Department, those who had a son serving in the British armed forces, or those about to emigrate overseas.

Those who didn't fit into those categories were inevitably attracted to the AMPC as a guaranteed way out. Anyone who expressed interest in enlisting was rewarded by being marched outside the barbed wire on a daily basis to receive drill instruction. For the duration of those exercises, the sergeant-major barked orders, taught them the basics expected of neophyte British soldiers, and allowed them to glimpse life on the other side of the fence. Then, once the lesson was over, they were marched straight back through the gates, reverting to the status of prisoners of His Majesty's government, an irony all too typical of the often odd nature of life at Hutchinson.

Eventually, the British army sent Captain Davidson, a salesman before the war, into the square to give the rest of the men the hard sell. Once he had gathered would-be recruits in a room, he would lock the door and tell them nobody could leave until they had signed up, or given him a good reason for not doing so. Fritz Hallgarten resented the forceful way the option was presented and decided against enlisting. His freedom would have to wait a little longer. Stent, however, signed on, took the oath of allegiance in the commandant's office, and even received the King's shilling (the token payment made to new soldiers by the British sovereign). All similarity to the normal process of joining the military ended at that particular point.

"You are now members of His Majesty's forces and subject to military discipline and military laws," said Commander Daniel in a speech to the new recruits. "But I am very sorry to inform you that there is no accommodation outside the camp for you on the island tonight. You will be taken tomorrow morning to Liverpool by ship and on to army barracks. Do you mind sleeping for one more night in the internment camp?"

What choice did they have? They returned to their houses on the square, going back to spend one more evening alongside the men with whom they had become fast friends. One last night for Ronald Stent to wonder how he'd ended up on this island, with a new name, serving a new country, and with the King's shilling in his pocket.

Rudolf Walter Stensch (the man who would become Ronald Stent) was born on February 9, 1914, in Berlin, a city with a then thriving Jewish population of over 200,000. His father, Georg Stensch, was a partner in a bronze statuary and lighting fittings factory, and when the world went to war that summer his company became a military subcontractor, producing artillery detonators for the Imperial German Army. His mother Elli (nee Karfunkelstein) was one of the first women in the city to get a license to drive. They were a prosperous family, and members of the Reformgemeinde temple on Johannisstrasse that preached a reformed version of the Judaic rite—the Sabbath shifted to Sunday, and prayers said in German.

While the Stensches were not especially religious, Rudi, as his family knew him, was fourteen when he first glimpsed the dark, anti-Semitic road Germany was heading down. In 1928, his uncle Hugo was set upon by Nazi thugs as he left the Berlin office of the Central Union of German Citizens of the Jewish Faith. The beating left him hospitalized for months. Five years later, the party to which his attackers were affiliated gained power in Germany. By then, Rudi was a student at Berlin's Humboldt University, where membership in a dueling fraternity earned him an invite to a remembrance service parade at the Unter den Linden opera house.

Stensch and five of his fraternity brothers were bemused by the invitation. They were Jewish, and that had already become enough to get them excluded from any major event. On this occasion, the sextet stood nervously through a ceremony involving President Paul von Hindenburg, Chancellor Adolf Hitler, and Reichstag president Hermann Göring. At one point in the proceedings, a photographer captured the three grandees standing together, and there in the background lurked a worried Stensch and his pals. The image was eventually turned into a postcard on which the six Jews were described as typical German students and, for decades afterward, Rudi joked about his missed opportunity to rid the world of the budding tyrant.

There was nothing funny about life for Jews from that point on, even those of a reformist faith like the Stensch family. As with many German students, Rudi's desire to sample different institutions took him to Bonn University to study law with a view toward becoming a judge one day. In 1934, he was told his Jewishness meant he could no longer attend classes. His academic career was over. But it seemed the Nazis had an alternative occupation in mind. His conscription papers arrived, and having passed a medical exam, he found himself on the brink of being called up.

"Which arm of the service do you want to go in?" asked the recruiting officer.

"Excuse me, sir, I am Jewish," said Stensch.

"Goodness gracious, you are a strong fellow!" said the officer, apparently ignoring his religious confession. "You are just the kind of man we want. I repeat again, what kind of service would you like to join?"

"The Luftwaffe," blurted Stensch, who hadn't even given the issue any thought.

Big mistake. Choosing the air force required him to sign up for five years rather than two, and they insisted he put pen to paper right there and then. As he continued to protest that his Jewishness prohibited him from enlisting, even citing his academic knowledge of the new laws, they ignored him. Within weeks a letter arrived formally accepting him into the Luftwaffe. This would have bothered Stensch more if he hadn't already resolved to leave Germany, setting his sights on England, where he had a promising connection.

His father did regular business with Basil Holroyd, whose family sold Lalique glass from a gallery on London's New Bond Street. The Englishman was just four years Rudi's senior, and during his visits to Berlin, the pair had become fast friends. The young German was intrigued by the visitor's appetite for having a good time in the bars and clubs once work was done.

Stensch's escape plan wasn't built on a desire to go and live somewhere free-spirited like the city that had spawned Holroyd. He wanted to move there to work because anything was more attractive than staying in Hitler's world. His father didn't like the idea, the elder Stensch still believing that Germany was bound to come to her senses and put a stop to the Nazi gallop before very long.

For anonymous members of society with financial means, getting to England was still relatively easy in 1934. Staying there, however, was a different matter. Basil Holroyd reckoned Rudi's best bet was to become a director in his company, a move that required investing money to secure working papers. Fortunately, Rudi's grandfather had just died and left him an inheritance that was the equivalent of £750, a substantial sum that fit the bill. The only problem with the scheme was that getting cash out of Berlin was by then a nearly impossible task.

At least, until they came up with a subterfuge to do exactly that.

"My father manufactured all sorts of lighting fittings and table lamps, including a series of animals," said Stent. "One was an elephant that was so large it had to be cast separately and was hollow on the inside. I ordered six of the elephants for Holroyd's. In my father's factory one night, [he] and his partner stuffed one elephant with money and placed it back among the six I had ordered."

When the ship carrying the cargo arrived in London, Stensch went to the docks to collect the particular elephant of the sextet that had a distinctive marking scratched on the heel. He couldn't take a chance on waiting to see if it would clear customs and excise. Once he had the object in hand, he hailed a taxi and climbed into the back, an excited, nervous wreck soon clawing at the piece as he tried to figure out how to open it.

Somewhere on a street in east London, the cab driver, also Jewish, grew tired of the harrumphing and asked his passenger what was going on. Stensch explained his predicament and the importance of the enormous elephant lamp. Sympathetic to his plight, the cabbie rooted around and found a giant spanner to hammer the animal. It cracked open to reveal £750 in Dutch guilders, the only foreign currency his father could find. Enough for Rudi to buy a share of the company and ensure his future in England, a country that he'd fallen in love with from his first visit as a teenage student.

"Most people's dream was to get into the States, [but] for me there was only one country, and that was England," said Stent. "England was the land of freedom. There were some aspects I didn't like, but [the] very fact you could stand up on a soap box at Speakers' Corner in Hyde Park and say what you liked [or didn't like] about the government [was a good thing]! Obviously, I didn't like the food, and those days, lager beer didn't exist in this country. It took me twenty years to get used to English bitter. There were many aspects—you didn't have central heating—these were minor things. I considered this the land of the free, and Germany was not the land of the free."

Rudi often pushed the pram containing Basil's infant son Michael (future biographer of George Bernard Shaw, among others) along Hammersmith Road, as his relationship with the Holroyds was as much personal as it was professional. Basil assisted him in a doomed, fanciful attempt to get Lloyd's of London to underwrite a scheme that would allow Rudi to bring his younger brother Gunther out of Berlin to a private school in Epping Forest. The pair also conspired on another smuggling venture, endeavoring to use the elephant ruse to get his sister's inheritance to her in London. On that occasion, a worker in the factory got wind of the plan and stole the cash before it left the warehouse in Germany.

Holroyd also advised him to change his name to something that didn't sound like the English word for a foul smell. And so Rudi Stensch became Ronald Stent. The German later credited his host family with educating him in what was expected of an Englishman and introducing him to a certain "upper-class lightheartedness and devil-may-care attitude," lessons often administered by Basil over lunchtime pints and sandwiches in the pub.

Stent returned to Germany briefly in 1936 with good purpose. On February 9, his twenty-second birthday, he married his girlfriend Gabi Teutsch in a joint wedding celebration that included the union of his sister Mausi and his college fraternity brother, Heinz Munsterberger. The party, held at the family's apartment on Kaiser Allee, was the last time all of them gathered together before fleeing Germany for Britain and the USA. Life in England was mostly good in those years, apart from the fact that he discovered the body of his aunt Katherina, who had killed herself with an overdose at her London flat in 1938.

The clouds were darkening over Europe by then. Gabi gave birth to Monica, their first child, in the middle of the Munich crisis. When war was finally declared the following year, Stent started to worry for the first time about being a German in Britain. Those concerns were exacerbated when he read some of the conspiracy theories about fifth columnists being promulgated by the newspapers of Rothermere and Beaverbrook, storylines that intensified following the invasions of Norway and the Netherlands. When he read speculation about whether the refugees from Hitler might be pretending to be Jewish, he sensed there was trouble ahead.

The war was a couple of months old when he was called to a tribunal to assess his status as an alien. He was asked to explain his presence in the country, his family background, and what organizations he belonged to. Unlike so many other foreigners who couldn't explain themselves to the retired magistrate usually adjudicating, the English he had perfected doing the *Daily Telegraph* crossword and listening to soliloquies at Speakers' Corner made his a straightforward case. Both he and Gabi were categorized as C, the lowest level, their only real restriction having to register with the local police.

Stent wanted to be more than a perceived interloper, though. He tried to join the British army, fostering a dream of sitting astride a white charger, riding through the Brandenburg Gate and shouting, "You bastards! I'm back again!" When the recruiters told him that at this point in the conflict he was only eligible for the AMPC, and wouldn't be allowed to carry a weapon, he thought better of it.

"I'm quite prepared to fight and die for this country, but I won't be a second-class soldier!" he said. Obviously, being interned later changed his mind on that score.

Still anxious to do his part, he became a voluntary ambulance driver, joining the Air Raid Protection Service, where he was taught first aid and lorry driving, roles that brought him into close contact with the police. In May 1940, one of the bobbies who knew him well called with some bad news. All foreigners living near RAF Northolt—a key airfield in the Battle of Britain—had to leave because the area had been declared a protected zone.

"How long have I got?" asked Stent.

"A week," replied the officer, who then gave him some advice. "All these places have been declared protected. You are persona non grata. Put your furniture into storage and find a friend who can give you some place to stay outside London."

The Stents had become good friends with the Hallgartens, fellow German exiles who had already evacuated out of London to Kings Langley in Hertfordshire. They were only too happy to open the doors of their new home to another family in distress. Any notions of enjoying life in this rural idyll were shattered a week into their stay by policemen, one in uniform, one in plainclothes, knocking on the door at dawn. They wished to search the house for any forbidden objects, a trawl that yielded a radio, a book of maps, and a map of the Tube. It was all very cordial until the officers told Fritz Hallgarten, "You might as well come with us to the station in Hemel Hempstead, because the inspector would like to talk to you there."

Mrs. Hallgarten saw the writing on the wall and demanded to know whether her husband was going to be interned. The police were adamant that this wasn't the case. He was just going to be required to answer some questions.

The subterfuge wasn't working, especially when the officers turned to Stent and told him he might as well come along, too.

At that point, their wives hastily started packing suitcases, even as one of the cops continued, inexplicably, to protest, saying, "It is really quite unnecessary. You will be home before the morning is out."

The whole affair was classically English and super polite. Mrs. Hallgarten asked the police if they'd mind driving the squad car to the end of the road, allowing Fritz and Stent to walk there to meet them. She didn't want the neighbors peering through their windows to think her husband was being arrested. They complied with the request.

This strange episode was followed by another incident that spoke to the truly peculiar nature of the internment business.

After departing the Hallgarten home, the two enemy aliens requested that the officers stop at a local store so they could stock up on chocolate, soap, and razor blades. Not a problem. The two Germans went shopping for necessities and then returned to custody.

It was the moment their car arrived at Hemel Hempstead station that Stent realized the worst. There were men sitting outside the building on top of their suitcases. Men with accents. Men just like him. They were not being brought in for questioning. They had been brought in to be interned.

As they waited around, he started talking to an old-timer, a septuagenarian who had been an inmate of Dachau, the poor man now dreading that something similar was about to happen in England. It was never going to be a camp of that nature, although they didn't know that when the army trucks pulled up and soldiers ushered them aboard.

The first stop on their journey was a territorial drill hall in Watford where barbed wire and fencing symbolized how the relationship between Britain and the people it had taken in had just changed. Dramatically.

"Nobody told us where we were going," said Stent. "The problem [was that] many of the people interned with us that day had been released after the Kristallnacht and had come to England from concentration camps in Germany. They were afraid the exact same thing was happening to them again, even after several months of freedom in England. My generation tried our best to cheer them up on these lorries, even though we had no idea what was happening."

Eventually, another fleet of trucks pulled up and parked, and three hundred more men boarded for the next leg of a magical mystery tour through southern England. Signposts had been removed in case of a German invasion, so as these vehicles trundled through the countryside, the passengers came up with conspiracy theories as to their final destination. Stent told Hallgarten they were probably headed to Southampton and ships bound for Canada or Australia.

Night was starting to fall when he spotted Windsor Castle and, shortly thereafter, the convoy pulled up outside a camp near Ascot.

Ordinarily, the facility served as winter quarters for the animals of the Bertram Mills' Circus, but it had been pressed into service earlier in the war to house German seamen. On this particular evening, the commandant had received no advance notice that he was supposed to be taking in internees, so he made them wait in the trucks outside while he sought confirmation. Nothing had been prepared for the new arrivals, the conditions so primitive that each man was given a bale of straw with which to stuff a makeshift mattress. Amid the chaos, Stent volunteered to get the moribund kitchen going so the newcomers could eat.

The three weeks in Ascot seemed longer because they were so insulated from the outside world. They had no idea what was going on. Their ignorance was such that Stent woke up each morning fearing that the Nazis might have invaded during the night, the British soldiers replaced by SS thugs. This explains why the milkman who delivered to the camp each day was beseeched to offer up information about the news of the war.

Finally convinced that the internees were enemies of Hitler rather than enemies of the British state, the commandant gave them a briefing one day that things were improving against the Germans. When he saw their positive response to this news, the entire tone of those in charge became more benevolent, and updates became regular.

Still, all were concerned about those they had left behind.

"Of all the hardships which we had perforce to bear, the total isolation at this most critical moment of the war was the hardest," wrote Stent. "Most of us had wives outside; many of them had to look after young children. They had no money. They were strangers, alone, with no family to whom they could turn, with no roots and few friends; it was weeks before they heard from us or us from them."

After three weeks in Ascot, they were on the move again, billeted for a couple of nights at Kempton Park Racecourse, where an altar was erected on the Tote for two rabbis to conduct a service on the Sabbath. From there, they were bound for Liverpool and, ultimately, the boat to the Isle of Man.

As they journeyed through north London on a train full of internees, Stent and Hallgarten realized from the stations they were passing through that this journey was taking them through Hertfordshire and near Kings Langley. In desperation, they hurriedly scribbled notes to their wives and dropped them out the window of the carriage, hoping that some passerby might pick up the letters and deliver them to Mrs. Hallgarten and Mrs. Stent.

If that turned out to be a romantic and forlorn hope, the move to Hutchinson Camp on the Isle of Man wasn't without its good fortune. As part of the first wave of inmates, Stent had a lot of downtime. One of his preferred ways to pass it was to stand by the gates to see the arrival of the new influx of refugees. He and others gathered there to see if they happened to know any of the fresh faces, and to press the newcomers for information—which again was initially difficult to come by behind barbed wire—about the war and the outside world.

"About three or four weeks after I arrived, I was standing there watching another troop lugging their suitcases up, and lo and behold, there was my father," said Stent. "He was absolutely amazed. I hadn't heard from him. He knew I was interned but had no idea where. The address my wife was writing to me at was an army post office. She knew I was on the Isle of Man, but she had no idea what camp I was in."

Georg Stensch had escaped Germany after Kristallnacht when he finally realized that the Nazi phenomenon wasn't going to dissipate. He moved to London with his second wife and was living in Maida Vale, an area with a large Jewish population, which meant that it took the authorities a while to get around to arresting him. Now, here he was, fifty-four years old, imprisoned, like all the others who had escaped the Nazi threat, by the country where they had sought refuge. For his son, his presence was, of course, an unlikely boon.

Then again, Stent's entire approach to his captivity differed from most of his peers. Although, like many, he had been leading a prosperous life now interrupted, he viewed internment as more of an opportunity than an oppression. His awe and wonder at getting to breathe the same air and share the same space with so many learned men and gifted artists dwarfed any lingering resentment at Great Britain—the country that just a few years earlier epitomized freedom, and was now taking away his liberty.

Even if the government regarded him as a security threat, he found Hutchinson to be a very stimulating environment. One afternoon, he found himself in a lecture on criminology given by Professor Max Grünhut. Seven years had passed since he'd been a student at Bonn University being taught the same subject by the very same man. Grünhut was forty-seven years old, had served as a military nurse in World War I, and had converted to Lutheranism to marry his wife. Nevertheless, his Jewish parentage had caused him to be dismissed from the chair of criminal law at Bonn at the school, and he'd emigrated to Oxford University, from whence he ended up at Hutchinson, now reuniting with a former student.

"By nature I'm an optimist so things don't go deep with me," said Stent. "That's my character. I hadn't gone through all the traumatic experiences of concentration camps; nothing really bad had happened to me up to that point. So, I think I suffered from all this far less than the majority of people who were there. I was also relatively young, twenty-five or twenty-six. I think also I felt I profited from my time there. First of all, I got to know people who could teach me an awful lot. It was like a university in itself. The older people all had university degrees. Secondly, I had to learn to put up with things. It was primitive and all that, I had to muster things. It was a very good indoctrination and apprenticeship for when I went into the army. I still think I do this, I try to pick out the things that are of positive value to me."

The morning after taking the oath of allegiance, Stent and the other new recruits were walked from the camp down to the port of Douglas. A ship took them back across the Irish Sea to Liverpool where they were handed their first British army uniforms. When they were dressed, they could only laugh at the irony. They were now wearing the clothes of the men who had spent the last four months guarding them at Hutchinson. "We were kitted out like our jailers!" recalled Stent. From there, they were taken to Bradford where 246 Company Pioneers was forming, its numbers made up of internees volunteering for the war effort, and, at last, Stent got access to a telephone and called Gabi down in Kings Langley.

"I was worried about my wife and my daughter," said Stent. "She was two years [old]. I was worried about them. I was not so much worried about myself."

He urged Gabi to come north to see him. She had no money to pay for a hotel. He had no money to give her to pay for a hotel. When she arrived, a local family put her up for free so the couple could reunite. An enemy alien no longer regarded as an enemy.

CHAPTER EIGHT

Barbed Wire University

Four men were sitting and lying on the lawn, all of them reading. . . .
Plato's Politics was in the hands of one of them, another read in its
original language Dante's Divine Comedy, whilst the expressions of
the last two showed all the joy caused by reading Goethe and Byron.
Overhead roared some planes safeguarding the blue sky against any
enemy actions; but surrounding the four readers the square burst with
bloom displaying the most vivacious colors and smells. Bypassers talked
thoughtfully of history, religion, philosophy, psychology, mathematics.
—KLAUS HINRICHSEN

IN NOVEMBER, 1938, JUST AFTER KRISTALLNACHT, THE VICE CHANCEL-
lor of Oxford University wrote a letter to Sir Ernest Holderness at the
Home Office. It was a plea for Paul Jacobsthal, university reader in Celtic
archaeology, to be granted permanent residence in England. Since his
arrival in April of 1936, the German professor had been staying in the
country on a series of one-year visas, and was growing increasingly concerned at the deteriorating situation back home. On January 2, 1939, the
Home Office finally declared there was now "no limit" to his stay.

Just eighteen months later, July 5, 1940, Jacobsthal was at his desk in
Christ Church College, working on a paper about Celtic geometric orna-
ments, when a plainclothes police officer knocked at the door, waving a
warrant for his arrest. He was shocked. Even though some of his émigré
colleagues had already been picked up in the sweeps since Churchill's

"Collar the lot!" declaration, he mistakenly believed his was a case of a different timbre.

"Had not the public Orator in 1937 at the Encaenia mentioned me as '*huius Universitatis non inquilinum, sed insitivum*'?" wrote Jacobsthal. "And had not Judge Dale presiding over the Tribunal, sifting Aliens, in October, 1939, addressed me, '. . . it is an honor for this country to have you here'?"

Those fulsome accolades counted for nothing now. Jacobsthal was able to summon the dean to try to intervene with the arresting officer on his behalf. They pled in vain for extra time so he could at least secure the various manuscripts and artefacts in his office. Instead, he left everything as it was, climbing into the waiting Black Maria which stopped at his house on Banbury Road so he could pick up his suitcase. By the time they reached the police station, he was sharing space in the back of the vehicle with Dr. Kosterlitz, a psychotherapist neighbor, another swept-up exile, clutching a beloved violin like a comfort blanket.

As the officers sifted through his bags (impounding his razor), Jacobsthal looked around and realized that the groups of men huddled together in custody represented a veritable who's who of exiled academics from the corners of Europe now ruled by Nazis. Some of them he knew personally, others just by reputation, and a few he would grow much closer to in captivity. There were professors of law, chemistry, history, music, Greek, and philosophy, drawn from the finest German and Austrian universities, men mostly chased out of their positions because of their Jewishness, men fortunate enough to find sanctuary and refuge at the various Oxford colleges. At least, until now.

The assembled dons were in various states of shock at the latest turn of events. Of them all, Jacobsthal perhaps should have been least surprised. Throughout the 1930s, the Nazis had been using archaeology (in a reprisal of an old tactic from World War I), and specifically, Celtic studies, as a means of spying. Alfred Mahr, director of the National Museum in Dublin, and a man often referred to as the father of Irish archaeology, was also head of the Nazi Party in that country. Jacobsthal had stayed at his house in Ireland in 1937. Far from offering protection, then, his academic connections actually brought him to the attention of increasingly paranoid authorities.

"A survey of recently released Home Office records suggests that Jacobsthal's presence in Britain was not without concern to the Home Office and MI5," wrote Katharina Ulmschneider and S. Crawford in *Prisoners of War*. "His letters, and letters about him, were under surveillance. Thanks to his contacts at Christ Church, Jacobsthal had high-ranking friends and supporters in England who put pressure on the Home Office before, during, and after his internment. Jacobsthal used his British contacts to the best of his advantage to make sure that his name was not on the 'enemy alien' list, though in the end his influence was not enough to override British suspicion about him."

John Beazley, professor of classical archaeology and art at Oxford, and close friend of Jacobsthal for more than a decade, soon turned up at the police station. Beazley had been instrumental in helping him to escape Germany and to secure a position at Christ Church and the presumed safety that came with it.

Although Jacobsthal's status as a veteran of World War I spared him when Hitler's Law for the Restoration of the Professional Civil Service in 1933 caused scores of Jewish academics to lose their jobs, he was actively engineering a move to England from that point on. Aside from the religious persecution, his specialization in Celtic art was in direct conflict with the National Socialists' erroneous assertion and official policy that the ancient Greeks had somehow been influenced by the ancient Germanics.

Having played a key role in helping his friend escape his homeland, Beazley now came bearing gifts, handing over chocolate, a pencil, an eraser, and a copy of *The Odyssey* published in 1899. Inside, the book was inscribed with the words *Tu ne cede malis, sed contra audacior ito*, meaning, "You should not give in to evils but proceed ever more boldly against them."

Jacobsthal subsequently used the writing materials Beazley gave him to record his trip through the internment system. After a night in Cowley Barracks, there followed a train journey to Devon, during which he encountered Thomas Armstrong, a colleague from Oxford, shocked to see Jacobsthal and other professors being marched along a station platform by soldiers with fixed bayonets. He then endured a week that felt like a month at the execrable Warth Mills, where he wrote on toilet paper for want of any other material.

Upon arrival at Hutchinson, he was placed in No. 24, where he shared a small back room with Dr. Egon Wellesz, an eminent musicologist, and Franz Pariser, an industrialist who had represented the interests of German clothing manufacturers at the Treaty of Versailles negotiations in 1919. While he thought of Wellesz as an intellectual equal whose career path was identical to his own, Jacobsthal also had great regard for Pariser. Although a businessman, his true passion was literature, impressing all the scholars around the square with his extensive knowledge of Michel de Montaigne and his ambition to one day write a book called *The Psychology and Physiology of Costume.*

While he enjoyed his daily conversations with Pariser, Jacobsthal looked down his nose at the way some of his fellow inmates quickly started to put together a rigorous and extensive schedule of lectures and classes in the camp. He scoffed at his housemate, Rudolf Pfeiffer, professor of philology in Munich and one of Europe's leading classicists, who attended morning meetings about the nascent education system being put in place. Rather than get involved, he derided this bold attempt to allow teachers to teach and residents to learn.

"There were some serious and very good lectures by people of our set who deemed it their duty to contribute, among them a masterly lecture by Pfeiffer on English Humanism, forming part of a cycle 'Aspects of English Life,'" wrote Jacobsthal. "But the majority of these lectures were cheap and delivered by dilettantes or conceited scholars, such as Professor L, who, to a dwindling audience, lectured for weeks on 'Philosophy of our Time,' or Dr. A. M., lecturing on the Bible, Christ, Philosophy, Economy, Astrology. He was the perfect type of an intellectual imposter, and I wonder who is guilty for his being a lecturer."

The ad hoc educational institution that Jacobsthal so cursorily dismissed was the brainchild of Bruno Ahrends and earned the camp its wider and most enduring reputation as a "university." Growing up in a wealthy Jewish family just outside Berlin, Ahrends dreamed of one day becoming a shipbuilder. When he discovered that his religion precluded him from that profession, even after he converted to Christianity, he became an architect of some renown. Among his most prominent Modernist designs was the 1931 *Weisse Stadt* housing development in Berlin-Reinickendorf, a building that is today a World Heritage Site. All of that impressive work, of course, counted for naught once Hitler took control.

Four years after his signature project was completed, Ahrends was no longer allowed to work as an architect in Germany, and he ended up in Britain via a stint in Italy. Among the first intake at Hutchinson, he was the main reason why, just forty-eight hours after the camp opened, lectures and classes were already available to interested internees. German prisoners of war during World War I had established a tradition of trying to put time in captivity to good use, but Ahrends could not have realized during the first days on the Isle of Man the caliber of individuals that would end up on the teaching roster of this particular facility, notwithstanding the refusal of Jacobsthal to lend his considerable weight.

On July 31, Ahrends chaired a meeting of the organizing committee, with Klaus Hinrichsen as secretary, of what the official stationery already called "Hutchinson Camp University." By that point classes were already under way in English, French, Spanish, Russian, and Italian; a roster of science lectures had been established; and among other subjects being covered were comparative religions, geography, music, law, medieval history, engineering, and architecture. In the interests of catering to the particular needs of the men, each of the forty-five houses had appointed a liaison officer to "communicate the wishes" of residents to those in charge. It was also announced that chess and gym tournaments were going to be organized, and a slate of gymnastics workouts was to be supervised by Ernst Boehm.

The logistics of what they put together so quickly, under such strained circumstances, are staggering. Over 150 different men taught more than 600 separate classes in the first six months. A remarkable number, given how at the beginning there were serious issues concerning space. To cater for demand many lectures had to be repeated for those who couldn't squeeze into improvised classrooms. In the first few weeks of that balmy summer, the lack of suitable venues was also solved by everybody crowding outside on different corners of the lawn, lecturers often perching on stone walls in front of their acolytes. So many took place so close together, however, that sometimes voices carried from one "classroom" to the next. Eventually, Commander Daniel organized the construction of a purpose-built hall.

Other simple obstacles had to be surmounted, too, the very necessities of any education institution being at a premium. There were, especially in the early days, never enough pens, pencils, typewriters, or sticks of chalk, and paper was the most sought-after commodity for teachers wanting to sketch outlines of lectures and students seeking to take notes.

Under the aegis of Ahrends—and later, Hinrichsen, his successor as de facto head of this university—the range of the curriculum was extensive and impressive. Among the litany of classes were agriculture, chemistry, overseas settlement, social sciences, film, history, photography, Russian, Greek, Latin, accountancy, shorthand, law, chess, and bookkeeping. Some attracted audiences as small as ten; others were witnessed by hundreds sitting in perfect silence on the grass outside.

"Day after day a huge crowd assembled on the lawn to listen to celebrities of international reputation and high academic standing, fellows of Oxford and Cambridge Colleges," wrote Hinrichsen. "Never before may they have had such a mixed audience, but scarcely ever had they had a more interested or eager one. And certainly most of them had never taught in such surroundings, in the open air with their eyes looking across towards the wonderful horizon of the sea. Several of the lectures felt this antique touch: they adjusted themselves to the unusual conditions. Others brought with them the college room air and simply recited the subjects they may have talked about often before—without being aware of the audience, and so much absorbed in thought, and so absentminded that one of them constantly addressed his audience as 'Ladies and Gentlemen.'"

What made it wonderful and special was that some of the least educated men in the camp suddenly had access to some of the most learned men in Europe, genuine luminaries in their fields. A board outside the post office updated the fresh academic additions to the calendar each day.

"We used to have a great many learned men in this camp, a few very important ones among them," wrote Heinrich Fraenkel. "One of those who hasn't [left] (though one of the best of all) gives [*sic*] us as fine a lecture on Plato as ever he held, the only difference being there are no Oxford undergraduates in the audience; there are mostly the kind of men described before, men, who used to earn their living with the same horny hands, now scribbling notes on Greek philosophy, or on political economics, for that matter, or a good many other subjects."

That the inmates were essentially spoiled for choice was not lost on Fred Uhlman.

"But our pride was our marvellous collection of more than thirty university professors and lecturers, mainly from Oxford and Cambridge, some of them men of international reputation. I doubt if one could have found a greater variety of lecturers anywhere else—we had an *embarras de richesses*," wrote Uhlman. "What could one do if Professor William Cohn's talk on the Chinese Theatre coincided with Egon Wellesz's Introduction to Byzantine Music? . . . Perhaps one felt more inclined to hear Zuntz on *The Odyssey* or Friedenthal on the Shakespearean stage. Every evening one could see the same procession of hundreds of internees each carrying his chair to one of the lectures, and the memory of all these men in pursuit of knowledge is one of the most moving and encouraging that I brought back from the strange microcosm in which I lived for so many months."

The commitment to excellence can be gleaned from Dr. Oskar Fehr spending days preparing a lecture that was ninety minutes long. Formerly chair of the eye department at Rudolf Virchov Hospital in Berlin, the sixty-nine-year-old was a leading ophthalmologist (the first to identify swimming pool conjunctivitis, among other achievements) whose escape from Germany was made possible by his friend, the legendary British spy Frank Foley. Fehr became the eye specialist for all of the camps on the island, yet when released was forced to take his medical exams again before being allowed to practice in Britain.

The diversity and quality of the lecturers is even more impressive given that some who could have helped, like Jacobsthal, were uninterested in fully contributing to the academic life of the place. A few esteemed professors may have been unwilling to teach because they felt they couldn't do so, at least to their own standard, without their notes or whatever slides they may have ordinarily used to illustrate their work. Others may have objected because they felt anything that normalized the camp life and experience could well prolong their incarceration there. Nonetheless, those who did volunteer played a key role in creating a uniquely convivial academic atmosphere that made time in incarceration not just tolerable but memorable for positive reasons. Social barriers dissolved.

"Fate unexpectedly threw us all together and forced a crowd of people of all classes and professions to live together peacefully in this strange make-believe world," wrote Gustav Hirschfeld, a civil servant in Hamburg before Hitler took over. "Professors can be seen talking confidentially to people who in normal circumstances would hardly be able to approach them. Men with plenty of money concern themselves with the trouble[s] of those who possess but little, and everybody endeavors to pass on to his fellow internees as much of his knowledge as possible. . . . Language teachers give lessons to people who perhaps never dreamt about speaking [anything] other than their mother tongue."

A sampling of the fare on offer illustrates the quality of what these men put together in these trying circumstances:

Dr. Gunter Zuntz, another of the great classicists, and future professor of Hellenistic Greek at Manchester University, taught "How the Bible Came Down to our Times."

Dr. Robert Eisler, a World War I veteran of the Austro-Hungarian Army who had spent time imprisoned in Dachau and Buchenwald, lectured about his seminal biography of Jesus.

Friedrich Burschell, German writer, literary scholar, and president of the international Thomas Mann Society, spoke about Faust.

Dr. Alfred Unger, playwright and author, delivered a series on Greek Philosophy.

Ahrends himself delivered a paper about "Why Town and Country Planning Is Indispensable." In between running the school, he also found time to write a position paper, replete with drawings, reimagining what the seaside town of Douglas might look like in the future. In a work that eerily predicts the eventual high-rise flavor of waterfront resorts all across southern Europe, he sketched a vision of the Isle of Man capital, where fifteen- to twenty-story apartment blocks replaced the Victorian hotels and B&Bs that he, ever the modernist, believed had "cluttered up the landscape."

"Don't forget we were to a large extent ex-university people, reading quite a lot, and exchanging books," said Fritz Hallgarten. "I remember the day a Jesuit priest gave us a lecture about the C or K in Caesar and Kaiser. There was not a subject in the world that wasn't discussed. I remember I gave a lecture about wine, so you really got some education in the camp. We had half a dozen rabbis, thirty professors, and the Jesuits; whatever question we wanted answered could be answered."

The presence of so many learned men lent itself to academic instruction and to personal growth, yet all of those college degrees counted for little when Dr. Zuntz received a package of daffodil bulbs from his wife Eva. She remained in Oxford raising their three children and had put the flowers in with the regular package of biscuits she sent him, with the intention that they could be grown to brighten up the surroundings of the camp.

"There was something wrong with the onions you sent," wrote Zuntz in a letter responding to the package. "They tasted awful."

Even if some, like Jacobsthal, chafed at how so many relished calling this impromptu education system a university, others did their best to replicate all aspects of normal campus life. In this respect, a debating society, a staple of all English colleges, was an inevitable addition to the cultural activities.

"It was a miracle of the human will," said Helmut Weissenborn, "to live and to work, changing a miserable prison camp into a kind of university."

There was a very practical side to the classes put in place, too. It wasn't all revisiting the classics. Some teenage inmates were anxious to finish their secondary education, which, in most cases, had been interrupted by fleeing one country or another.

"We wanted to usefully use the time while we were interned to further our education," said Freddy Godshaw, known as Adolf Gottschalk when he arrived in England as a sixteen-year-old refugee from Germany in August 1939. "Every other person in the camp was a doctor of something or other. We soon had a timetable and had lessons every morning. I only wish I would have kept one of those timetables, as there were lessons from Chinese and all languages any one ever wanted to learn, and every other subject, too. I always will remember our maths teacher. He was a professor who had not taught any basic maths since his early days as a teacher. Apparently it took him a long time to prepare his lessons each day, as he had forgotten all his early training."

The "university" also proved to be adaptable and open to change. Following an influx of men from farming backgrounds in September, many arriving from Prees Heath in Shropshire, a syllabus was immediately created to cater to their specific needs, promising "to give young farmers an opportunity to increase their knowledge in cultivation of soil, stock-breeding, botany, and manuring."

A world removed from that sort of pragmatic instruction, there existed within the camp a private society of the most learned gentlemen, a sort of underground intellectual movement. At night in various houses, sometimes in bedrooms, groups gathered to discuss books and other topics.

Even one of those personally responsible for turning the university into such a robust institution relished the opportunity to get up close and breathe the same air as these intellectual giants on those occasions.

"And then there were some wonderful nights when a small group of us assembled in one of the narrow bedrooms to listen to the more private talk of a man who outside the wire used to be world-famous for his publications, who, however, inside the camp was nothing but a friend," wrote Hinrichsen. "And yet another group read and studied *The Odyssey* under the leadership of classical scholars, and some of them may have compared their fate with that of the immortal ancient fighter and traveler, Odysseus."

Of course, these soirees were much more to Jacobsthal's liking.

"The better part of spiritual life was going on in private, unorganized," he wrote. "And No. 24 was the respected and much envied center. Every night after dinner and roll call, we put our two tables in the common room together, covered the windows with embezzled blankets, and screened the stolen bulb with a cover of an old photographic camera which Cohn had discovered in a rubbish heap in the basement. Lecture and discussion went on until 10:15 [p.m.], when the Air Raid Warden furiously knocked at the window: 'Put your bloody lights out!'

"For weeks on every second night, Pfeiffer interpreted *The Odyssey*; for a long time, before the Clarendon Press furnished us with a real classical library and even with a Liddel-Scott, Beazley's *Odyssey* [gifted to Jacobsthal at the police station the day of his arrest] was the only text we had. I was certainly the most grateful among the audience, for I have read Homer twice during these months with a pleasure and an intensity as hardly ever before."

Inevitably, given the caliber of people at these more select gatherings, the range of topics discussed indicates that these were venues that hosted an exchange of ideas on a more intimate level. Dr. Karl Forchheimer, an economist, one-time head of the Austrian Ministry of Labour and late of Oxford University, spoke about unemployment and the trade cycle. Wellesz gave lectures on topics such as the genesis of an opera. Professor Hans Rothfels, former chair of history at the University of Konigsberg and late of St. John's College, Oxford, held forth on Bismarck, about whom he'd written one of the definitive biographies. Professor Emil Goldman, once of the University of Vienna, lectured on Etruscan philology, while Count Graf Mattuschka, a Prussian nobleman, recited his poetry.

"Those evenings were a serious matter and prevented boredom and pointless talk," wrote Jacobsthal. "I sometimes felt reminded of people on a polar expedition."

Dr. Gerhard Bersu was regarded as something of a permanent guest at No. 24, the house that Jacobsthal believed to be the unofficial intellectual hub of the camp. That Bersu, who also lectured in the camp university, would be welcome in that elite company and obviously respected by

Jacobsthal made complete sense. His résumé was so impressive that even the heavyweight academics who gathered there after dark were willing to sit through him giving them "an introduction to prehistory" lecture one evening. No matter what subject they specialized in, they realized here was one of the preeminent archaeologists of the time in their midst.

Bersu was born in modern-day Poland in 1889. His father was a Jewish manufacturer. As a teenager he was obsessed with digging up the past and, by eighteen, was working as an assistant at excavations near Potsdam, under the tutelage of Carl Schuchhardt, the most celebrated German archaeologist of the era. By the time World War I broke out, Bersu had carved out a reputation of his own and was appointed officer for the protection of monuments and collections in occupied France and Belgium. After the conflict ended, he was centrally involved in organizing the repatriation of cultural artefacts.

During the 1920s, Bersu started working for the German Archaeological Institute and conducted a famous excavation at the Nördlinger Ries in Bavaria. He became director of the institute by 1931, and under his leadership it became a hive of scholarship. Along the way, he met and married Maria Goltermann, who had a PhD in art theory and specialized in the Germanic-Roman period. Her husband's rather seamless career progression was rudely interrupted by the rise of Hitler. Bersu's service to his country in World War I counted for little then, because the new leader of Germany and his acolytes had a particular interest in rewriting the nation's archaeological history for their own ends.

"The Minister of the Interior's guidelines also included teaching how the Germanic race (superior in culture and language) was distributed in prehistory based on artifacts," wrote Megan Young in *The Nazis' Archaeology*. "He provided the following examples to support his argument that all great European and Near Eastern civilizations owed their development to the Germanic race. He claims that archaeological evidence points to German invasions of Asia, North Africa, and Egypt as early as the 5th millennium BC, resulting in the advanced Indians, Medes, Persians, and Hittites all being descendants of the Germanic race. In addition, the ruling classes of the later great Greek and Roman civilizations were Germanic."

Unlike many of his peers whose objections to this ridiculous stuff faded quickly when they saw how much money the Nazi regime was willing to invest in archaeology to further its political aims, Bersu could not be bought. He refused to renege on his life's work and to conform to these ludicrous attempts to distort prehistory in order to further Hitler's theories of racial superiority. That stance, and his Jewish heritage, led to him being demoted from director of the Römisch-Germanische Kommission to the post of excavation officer in 1935, and he was forced to retire altogether two years later.

Fortunately, his reputation was by that point international. An Honorary Fellow of the Society of Antiquaries of London in 1933, he had developed a personal and professional relationship with O. G. S. Crawford, the aerial photographer. As president of the Prehistoric Society, Crawford engineered an opportunity for Bersu and his wife Maria to excavate an Iron Age site at Little Woodbury in Wiltshire in the summers of 1938 and 1939. There, Bersu introduced a modern continental approach to digging, and when war broke out in September 1939, the couple failed (or pretended to fail) to make a ferry home and became refugees.

They were both interned on the Isle of Man, but it was several weeks before Bersu learned that Maria was an inmate at Rushen, ten miles away. There were so many couples and families split up in this way that, in October of 1940, the authorities decided to facilitate weekly meetings in local hotels where husbands could spend half an hour with their wives and children. Even still, the rules of engagement were strict.

"Communication must be entirely verbal," stated the notice advertising a meeting at the Ballaqueeney Hotel in Port St. Mary. "No money, documents, letters or parcels must be exchanged. If any internee disobeys these instructions, the whole scheme will be stopped immediately."

As per one account, the men arrived first to whichever hotel ballroom was booked for that week. They then were tasked with setting up tables and chairs all over the dance floor. When their wives finally arrived, the husbands rose from their seats and applauded the women to their tables. While couples discussed their plans to gain release, the Bersus may have spent their thirty minutes together talking shop and plotting some way to make life on the Isle of Man more tolerable.

Eventually, Bersu persuaded Commander Daniel that his expertise at excavating might be put to good work, prospecting for manganese ore, a metal much sought after in the war effort. Obviously acknowledging that here was a man with unique knowledge of digging up the earth, Daniel bought into the idea. Soon, Bersu was leading a group of fellow internees under armed guard through the barbed wire and deep into the countryside, a boon some of them greatly appreciated.

"Go mining with Dr. Bersu," wrote Fred Uhlman in his diary for November 4, 1940, of an expedition that centered around St. Patrick's Chair in the south of the island. "For manganese. Wonderful day and delightful landscape. Mountains rather in the mist just like in Grasse or in the Var valley. Amazing sunset."

Eventually, word reached Eleanor Megaw, the visionary acting director of the Manx Museum, that no less a personage than Bersu was behind barbed wire in her town. Aware of his standing, she came up with the idea of putting him to even smarter use than trawling for manganese. Having persuaded the relevant authorities, she later organized a series of digs in which Bersu and Maria (by then reunited as a couple at the Port St. Mary camp) led a team of inmates each day to excavate round mounds at Ballacagan and Ballanorris.

Those days were so productive that Bersu remained on the island after the war ended, and two decades later, published a book of his findings, *Three Viking Graves in the Isle of Man*, a work that fundamentally altered scholars' understanding of the Iron Age in the region.

Hermann Fechenbach.
(COURTESY OF PATRICK MOONEY)

Fechenbach at work.
(COURTESY OF PATRICK MOONEY)

Adolf Mirecki.
(COURTESY OF DANIEL MIRECKI)

Hutchinson Camp residents gather before an outing to meet their wives, who were in other camps.
(TATE GALLERY)

Hellmuth Weissenborn working at a desk at Hutchinson Internment Camp.
(TATE GALLERY)

Internees marveling at the work in the Camp's first art exhibition.
(TATE GALLERY)

Commander H. O. Daniel, the man who wanted the Camp to be an exemplar.
(TATE GALLERY)

Internees collecting rations to be brought back to each house.
(TATE GALLERY)

Hans Brick (aka, Johann Neunzer), a lion tamer and animal wrangler, sitting by the window into which he had scratched images of some of his favorite creatures.
(TATE GALLERY)

Paul Hamann, right, and Peter Fleischmann (later named Midgley), working on a small carved figure.

(TATE GALLERY)

A soldier stands sentry in Hutchinson Square.

(TATE GALLERY)

Postcard featuring a portrait of Fred Uhlman, by Kurt Schwitters.
(TATE GALLERY)

Morning roll call when internees lined up outside each house to be counted.

Hans Furth and family after the war.

CHAPTER NINE

Technically Speaking, a Spy

The Technical School was founded to replace aimlessness with a purpose. The purpose is to train these people who wish for release more than anything else and who yet, once they are released, would not know where to go and what to do because they would find themselves cut off from the very roots of what used to be their roots in life. We want to mould them into men, who will be able to stand up for themselves, and who can offer their new country useful service and fight for it; we, the technicians and engineers of the Technical School, are preparing the weapons for this fight, and we are teaching all those who are willing to learn how to use them.
—LUDWIG WARSCHAUER, *THE CAMP*, ISSUE NO. 2,
SEPTEMBER 29, 1940

ON JULY 13, 1940, AS THE NEW RESIDENTS OF HUTCHINSON SQUARE arrived, Regimental Sergeant-Major Potterton was charged with the task of dividing the intake up into groups of thirty and assigning them to houses. Klaus Hinrichsen found himself put in with a typical motley crew. For instance, a man in a gold-buttoned blazer, that somebody whispered had once been a prominent journalist in Berlin, was appointed his House Father. His main qualification, Hinrichsen deduced later, was that Potterton figured his smart dress sense marked him out as leadership material.

Somebody else caught Hinrichsen's eye that evening—not so much for his clothes, but for his attitude. As everybody else shuffled about diffidently, evincing an air of concern and dread about their new surroundings, a rather rotund character in his early fifties cut a very different jib. With a pipe perched in his mouth, wearing a track suit, and apparently unencumbered by a single suitcase, this man was laughing aloud at the nature of his predicament. The thought of living behind barbed wire on an island in the middle of the Irish Sea was not in the slightest bit unnerving. In fact, to him, it was kind of funny.

"He told all and sundry, with a pervading chuckle," wrote Hinrichsen, "about the consternation bordering on panic when various ministries in London and war-important industries elsewhere would discover that he had not turned up for a second day. He threw around an impressive assembly of political and industrial names who were intimate friends of his and would scour the British Isles to locate him. Just as a joke, he said, he would keep silent for one more day, after which, surely, the Commander would be urgently requested to send him back to London by the next available boat."

At least, Hinrichsen surmised, that optimistic take on his present circumstances explained why this strange individual hadn't bothered to bring any luggage with him. Obviously, he wasn't expecting his stay to be a lengthy one. True to form, next morning, the pipe-smoking big noise, who went by the name Ludwig Warschauer, requested a formal meeting with Commander Daniel. A brazen move befitting somebody who believed they were of a stature too large to be imprisoned at Hutchinson. And one that apparently impressed Daniel so much that he immediately sent more than one telegram to the authorities in London on Warschauer's behalf, the type of special treatment afforded few prisoners.

The morning after that first meeting, Hinrichsen caught an up-close glimpse of the true extent of this odd character's burgeoning influence. When he came downstairs, he discovered Warschauer sitting in a kitchen chair being carefully shaved by another internee. At the stove, the house cook was busy preparing the bizarrely esteemed guest a delicious smelling breakfast of bacon, eggs, and toast, all three parts of the meal having been secured by bribing a British soldier through the barbed wire to deliver the contraband. This, truly, was a man apart.

The troubling tableau was completed by the House Father sitting across the table. The once distinguished journalist was now fulfilling the role of diligent personal secretary, busily taking notes as Warschauer dictated the contents for a plethora of fresh, urgent letters and telegrams he needed to be translated into English and immediately dispatched to people in power. By his side through all of this was a rather sinister-looking character who, it later emerged, had been retained as Warschauer's personal bodyguard.

Hinrichsen and the other residents were disturbed by what they had seen. Who was this man? Why was he acting like this? Why was the house captain so servile toward him? And where did he get the means to employ his own minder? These questions were flying around the house and then the camp all that morning. In a setting where everybody, regardless of background, occupation, or reputation, was now supposed to be regarded as more or less equal, Warschauer was acting like a de facto commanding officer, a man somehow superior.

"By lunchtime, reports about this scene and the servile and conniving attitude of our house captain had spread," wrote Hinrichsen. "There was a motion for a vote of no confidence, he resigned, and, to my surprise, since I was rather younger than the majority of the inmates of the house, I was elected. By evening, my predecessor had moved out."

The swift manner in which the House Father was deposed and replaced illustrates how quickly camp residents had started to adhere to political structures and democratic machinery. But he was only a bit player in this particular story, a casualty of the peculiar presence that was Ludwig Warschauer. The mystery about his character and provenance deepened when he quickly informed his housemates that he too would be moving out. Not out of the camp, as he had boasted on the day of arrival—merely out of their building.

Even though the various telegrams and letters he sent to grandees, political and industrial, presumably went unanswered, Commander Daniel was so impressed by Warschauer's spiel about his background in engineering that he gave Warschauer complete control of No. 36, an as yet unoccupied building. His task was to turn it into a Technical School where inmates could receive practical training for future employment as electricians, wireless engineers, and radio technicians. Warschauer was appointed headmaster.

This rapid-fire promotion to a position of some power and influence—his job gave him his own lodgings within the school building and a staff working beneath him—intensified the rumors swirling around Hutchinson Camp about Warschauer. He added to the speculation himself by refusing to confirm whether he was even Jewish. A strange move in a camp where 80 percent of residents were of the faith, it may have been a defensive measure to throw his real identity into doubt.

As soon as he became one of the most talked-about prisoners in the place, some inmates from engineering backgrounds said they recognized him as a Berliner Jew who had gained special privileges from the Gestapo, even being allowed to drive a car after that was forbidden under the Nazis in 1938. Communist internees told similar tales, alleging his special status had been afforded as a reward for him deploying his extensive engineering skills to help the Nazis monitor the phones of people under suspicion.

"He started the school and called himself principal," said Freddy Godshaw, one of the first students to move into the Technical School. "He was quite a character. . . . One never quite believed all his stories."

These stories were bolstered by corroborating evidence from former members of the German communist party when they arrived in camp. These allegations were, inevitably, accompanied by more obvious questions. Was he there as a Nazi fifth columnist? Was he spying on them even now? Is that why he had been sent to the island?

As the rest of the Hutchinson community tried to get to the bottom of the various tall tales, Warschauer appeared nonplussed by all the fuss. Still openly asserting to anybody who'd listen that he was a man of great influence, he styled himself as an individual who arrived in England in 1939 bearing letters of introduction to a slew of prominent British politicians and industrialists. The more he spoke, the more innuendo there was about him and the more difficult it became to separate fact from fiction.

This had, apparently, been a problem for a long time around Warschauer, and would remain a difficulty for both his fellow inmates and the London authorities for some time yet.

According to the passport with which he arrived in England, Ludwig Max Israel Warschauer was born in Posen (then a province of Prussia) on February 14, 1898. His family was Jewish, solidly middle class and respectable, his father having served as *Geheimrat* (trusted adviser) in the city of Danzig (also Prussian territory at the time). In his late teens, Warschauer fought in World War I, and in the chaos that ensued in the aftermath of the Treaty of Versailles, was a member of the Berlin Freikorps, a right-wing, paramilitary group where many disillusioned, demobbed soldiers found an outlet for their various frustrations.

"[Warschauer's] character was destroyed by the war and he was even expelled from the Freikorps for having interfered with the petty cash," according to an MI5 biography. "Thereafter, his parents sent him to a sanatorium where they hoped he might be cured of his inability to distinguish between truth and lies. In the post-war, some of his posts he is said to have lost because of financial irregularities."

Although his questionable relationship with facts made it difficult for anybody, even MI5, to piece together a completely reliable version of Warschauer's biography, he did gain some qualification as an engineer in the early 1920s. In that role, he served an internship at AKG Berlin, and had stints at several other reputable companies, including Siemens. During this phase of his life, he ended up in the Middle East where he was retained overseeing wireless work for the Anglo-Palestine Bank in Jaffa and, indeed, dealt with His Majesty's Postmaster General in Palestine regarding the technical requirements for a radio broadcasting license there.

Like so much else in his professional and personal life, his sojourn in the Middle East ended badly. In his own telling, his prosperous career there was derailed by his first wife Miriam destroying his reputation in the industry before their marriage was annulled in a Tel Aviv court. Back in Germany, he picked up the pieces and, for a time, claimed to have owned, or partly owned, an electrical company he later said was taken from him when the Nazis banned Jews from business.

Sometime around 1935, he started working with Dr. Karl Daniel, a brilliant Cologne-based engineer who had invented the "Tefifon," a machine capable of making sound recordings of any length without the knowledge of the subject. Exactly the type of cutting-edge technology the increasingly paranoid, intrusive Nazi regime was interested in, Warschauer secured the license to sell the Tefi machines in territories outside Germany. At least, he said he did.

His biography constantly distorted by his own exaggerations, he also professed to have been in partnership with the inventor, rather than just working for him as a contracted sales representative. In the latter guise, he did travel outside of Germany, a commercial activity that brought him to the attention of the Nazi authorities. Citing a potential breach of the currency laws as the reason for their sudden interest in him, the Gestapo brought Warschauer in for questioning. What subsequently happened in the interview room is, of course, a matter of conjecture. His own story was that they roughed him up and threatened him. Others differ.

"In fact, Warschauer received no ill-treatment from the Gestapo other than the anti-Semitic abuse which was common form," went a report in MI5. "He seems to have enjoyed some immunity as a '*Frontkämpfer*' [a former soldier who had fought on the front lines] and still more as a past member of the Freikorps. For those reasons and because of his character, Warschauer was probably marked down as a passable espionage agent. Indeed, his visits to the Gestapo were possibly part of a recruiting campaign."

While it's difficult to pinpoint exactly how he managed to avoid the fate of so many other Jews questioned by the Gestapo in Berlin, one episode, straight from the "how to groom a spy" handbook, offers obvious clues. Following a particularly agitated interview with the Gestapo at the end of 1938, they informed him he was being released because an old friend of his had intervened on his behalf and was now waiting for him back at his apartment.

The old friend was, indeed, already at his place when he arrived home. The problem was he'd never seen this man, a character called Hans Sauer, before. Sauer claimed they had soldiered together in the Freikorps in Berlin nearly two decades earlier and was able to relate to Warschauer intimate details of his own life. He also alleged that his own aristocratic background and contacts in the War Office equipped him to help his stricken Jewish colleague in his hour of need. The grooming had begun.

Over several meetings, Sauer upped the ante. He told Warschauer he'd vouched for his good character with the Nazis and was working toward securing an exit permit so that Warschauer and his fiancée could leave Germany. All he wanted in return was for his old friend to establish business contacts in Poland in order to sell the Tefi equipment. This would provide the perfect cover for him to conduct some espionage about airfields, power stations, and factories. To throw the Poles off the scent, in a rather convoluted arrangement, Warschauer was to use a British base for the company.

"Shortly before his departure, Sauer gave him cover addresses in Stockholm, Copenhagen, and Amsterdam, which he was to use for correspondence from Poland," reported MI5. "He also gave him a bottle of secret ink and a bottle of developer, and in addition gave him special camera films which were colour films disguised as ordinary films. The idea of this was that, if they were caught in the post, the negatives would be ruined by faulty development and it would not be possible to tell what subjects had been photographed. . . . [H]e was also told that he could obtain new supplies of these films from the AGFA branch in Warsaw."

Warschauer never reached Poland and was probably never meant to. The problem with his elaborate story about Sauer is that it omitted the crucial fact that his English work visa was actually secured following a concerted campaign on his behalf by Leon Ignace Bergl, a Hungarian-born businessman and another employee of WAF Co. Ltd., the company established to distribute Daniel's invention. Bergl had brought the Tefi machine to London where he demonstrated it to, among others, Scotland Yard, and he told authorities that producing it in a factory in England would require the technical expertise and crucial presence of his colleague, Ludwig Warschauer.

In his application to the Home Office, Bergl also pointed out that it was a matter of great urgency due to the deteriorating situation for Jews in Germany and, as an added incentive, claimed Yugoslavia was anxious to get Warschauer to bring his communications and engineering know-how to Belgrade. Whether through bribery as he asserted or the machinations of the Gestapo, Warschauer's visa for England was granted by the British Embassy in Berlin on June 20, 1939, and he was processed by immigration at Croydon six days later. Of course, befitting his flair for the dramatic and plausibly fictitious, he painted the circumstances of his departure in more heroic terms.

"When I met Elisabeth Koshen, I was deeply infatuated by her, and when she agreed to marry me, my entire life seemed to brighten up," wrote Warschauer during his internment. "But my father-in-law, his wife, and my fiancée had committed a heavy offence against the foreign currency law by being silent partners in a Dutch company. Through Hans Kampinsky, owner of the London restaurant who also was a partner of this business deal, and who is in urgent need of capital, had disclosed in London the true facts of this partnership, the whole matter had come to the ears of some German officials. The immediate arrest of my fiancée, her parents, and her cousin was already considered. Through my connections with Dr. Hortsmann and Mr. Sauer, I managed to delay any action especially by different payments of sums totalling 40,000 M [Reichsmarks—a sum then worth about $16,000] to some minor officials. This money was paid to me by Dr. Karl Daniel as part of my partnership in his invention. Then I managed to get the parents out of Germany, then her children, then myself and, at last, her."

There was a kernel of truth in this, but, then again, he also claimed outlandishly to have clashed forty times with the Gestapo and somehow lived to tell the tale.

Warschauer married Elisabeth, mother of two children from a previous marriage, on August 10, 1939, in London. In terms of establishing the WAF company in England, he had achieved very little by the time he was interned in 1940. Indeed, as late as 1942, WAF, despite the presence of Herbert Williams, a Conservative MP for Croydon South, as chairman of its board, was described by British intelligence as nothing more than a skeleton operation.

Still, Warschauer's involvement with Tefi, his past as an engineer, and his ability to talk up his résumé greatly impressed Commander Daniel. On August 22, 1940, just five weeks after arriving at Hutchinson as just one more internee, Warschauer delivered a speech marking the opening of the camp's Technical School, where he was now headmaster.

"Today we are starting the Technical School for engineers, thanks to the help and understanding of the commander of this camp," he said. "We must be quite aware of the fact that this is an experiment. But what is an experiment to an engineer? When does a real engineer undertake an experiment? Only when he believes in his success, when the experiment represents something new, be it an invention or a construction, when he feels that he can replace something imperfect or inferior by a thing more perfect and more useful."

From there, he pivoted to tell the story of how the Tefi machine was created, inevitably exaggerating his own role in its creation, extolling its contribution to the British war effort and reminding the students that great things can only be achieved through trial and error. Then, he waxed lyrical about how he was inspired to start the school out of a desire to give so many idle young men a greater purpose through training that would serve them and their adopted country well upon release. With typical bombast he speculated that the success of the project in this camp would cause it to be replicated elsewhere.

"I want to explain in a few words the plan on which we are going to work," he said. "Our intention is to provide those who take part in our courses with the basic theoretical knowledge which is necessary, and then to start with the practical work. But that is only a beginning. The practical work will start in earnest when I have returned to London to resume there my work as the technical manager of an English industrial undertaking. I shall then be in position to send you practical material which has been carefully selected.

"The funds for this will be provided both by my friends and myself, and once you have got those materials here in the camp, the experiment will have to cease to be an experiment. If we base our efforts on the will to teach and to learn and carry out practical work in the same spirit, then the initial success is guaranteed. I am convinced that the commandant of this camp will be just as prepared to help us exploit this initial success as he was prepared to help us start at all, for the benefit of this camp, for the future of the internees and, as we all hope, for the success of the country."

The irony of Warschauer's line about doing his bit for the success of England was not lost on those in the audience that day who regarded him with great suspicion, and who, without access to his substantial MI5 file, believed he was, indeed, a spy. Their skepticism didn't matter a jot because Commander Daniel bought completely into his in-house visionary's idea of what the Technical School could be. Was the man in charge duped by the German's ability to sell the concept, or was he merely delighted that a facility such as this might offer prisoners one more way of passing the time productively? Probably a bit of both.

Fred Uhlman was not impressed, describing Warschauer as Daniel's "blue-eyed boy" and "pet internee." To him and the majority of others, nothing about the Technical School's headmaster's origin story added up. Too many others in camp had versions of his biography in which he'd assisted the Gestapo. They could only smile wryly at his grandiloquent assertions about wanting to assist the British in their war effort, suspecting (quite rightly, as it turned out) that he had been part of a nefarious plot to do the opposite just months earlier.

"There was a man," said Rudolf Munster, the first Camp Father, in his recounting of Warschauer. "And there was a suspicion, that somehow or other [although he was Jewish], that he was a double agent. There was no confirmation of that and I think the suspicion was unfounded and he'd been done [an] injustice. But we had to watch him for quite a long time because of this. Further details I don't know, because this sort [of] thing came all the way up from the British administration, and they said, 'This man has got to be watched.'"

None of that mattered unduly to Daniel, who ensured that Warschauer's star rose quickly and stayed aloft. Within three days of the school opening, there were 170 students enrolled, and at a meeting of the camp committee, the would-be industrial spy was now listed as "Dr.," and had the letters "Dip Eng" (Diploma in Engineering) appended to his name. Was he a doctor, or was he just affecting the title given that every other person at the meeting seemed to be a professor? Most likely the latter.

Blurring the lines of his biography didn't impact on his standing with the powers that be—especially since he had done such a good job of establishing the new institution that it was favorably mentioned in *The Guardian* in an article about life in the internment camps. This positive reference no doubt did wonders for Warschauer's standing with Daniel, who, of course, always felt in competition with other establishments on the island. With pupils and teachers living in the same house, Warschauer boasted that it was run like a top boarding school, and, in fine weather, even insisted on physical training for all students, at seven in the morning. There were classes in mathematics, physics, electricity, installation, technical drawing, technical translation, and, most crucially, English—which he insisted was the only language to be heard in the building. Homework, too, was a staple.

"I was lecturing on how to replace a fuse, how to replace switches and things like that in English," said Richard Simon, who taught classes on electrical installations, despite the fact that he'd only completed his electrician's apprenticeship earlier that year. "I spoke perfect English. Not many people did, but I did. So people came to my lectures in masses. [They] didn't really want to learn, they just wanted to hear English spoken. . . . A little bit [of equipment] came in from the Quakers—wires, switches, switchbacks, and old pieces like that. I didn't write to them, the management did. I was not in the management. I only did what I was told, to speak for half an hour . . . on electrical safety or something like that. . . . We did it, people came, people had lessons in mathematics, electrical engineering, machinery, and all sorts of things. Marvellous. I did insulation. . . . Eighty or a hundred people came to a lecture."

Just over a month after it opened, the second issue of *The Camp* newspaper announced that henceforth an amount of space in the publication would be given over to a regular update on the activities of the Technical School. The first such article was another Warschauer manifesto, one more party political broadcast on his own behalf.

> *We, the internees of this camp, are uniting; we are uniting for our release, and we are waiting for the victory of this country in its struggle against Nazidom. . . .*
>
> *It is not that we want new pupils. We have already got more than one hundred and fifty, who attend daily and regularly, and that*

is about as many as the school can deal with. Yet, we are trying all the time to extend the scope of the school and to find new opportunities for working and learning. It is for this reason that we have called together all the technicians, engineers, and chemists of this camp so that all the talent available may be used.

But we must demand and insist that our plan, which took shape in most difficult circumstances, which was carried through in spite of indifference, the skepticism and the opposition of many—that this plan should be supported by the whole camp; that the whole camp should contribute to it being a full success.

We attack! We attack all those who waste their time and try to waste ours in useless debates and discussions, who resign themselves to fatalistic inactivity.

We attack all those who, untruthfully, deny that valuable work is being done here and that even behind barbed wire one can work for the victory of this country and the defeat of the Nazis.

We attack all those who withdraw, grumbling and dissatisfied; we shall not tire of working for what we consider to be the right way.

To be an engineer is to act, not to talk. It is by action only that one can obtain one's object in life.

We wish for release, but while we are waiting for release we want to spend our time in a way which will convince the British Government and the British people that the men in this camp are their friends, worthy to be accepted into their ranks.

By the fourth issue of *The Camp*, Warschauer had given up the pontificating and his attempts to persuade everybody he was fighting the good fight against Nazism. Instead, he opted for a striking advertisement. Afforded a whole page in the publication, he decided to issue a brief call to arms backgrounded by white space and a black outline. The design definitely caught the eye, even if the message was a familiar riff.

"Teaching and learning, training and working, are better for your release and your future existence than any grumbling and complaining. Don't you share this attitude? Then why don't you join the Technical School!"

Plenty of the younger, unqualified internees did join, many because it simply gave them something to do. Others joined because Warschauer assured all and sundry that every graduate would be able to procure gainful employment in one of his engineering companies once they were released and/or the war was over. He didn't mention that WAF was not even a going concern at that point. That was only the fine print of the arrangement, not something desperate men were liable to concern themselves with.

"Hope runs high among people whose first attempts to establish themselves in their homeland [have] been frustrated by internment," wrote Hinrichsen. "And, of course, once free, he would work tirelessly for the release of his new friends. His new-found Technical School attracted many youngsters, but also gained a reputation as a sweatshop where the pupils had to split mica instead of getting lessons. Yet others expressed gratitude for the training received and have found well-paid jobs."

The air of mystery around the school's director was amplified on occasion when deputations of officials from London arrived at the camp and were sequestered for long spells with Warschauer in Commander Daniel's office. The other men had no idea who these characters in suits were or why they had come, but their recurring presence turbo-boosted the chatter about the engineering wizard's true identity and exact purpose among them.

Other incidents amplified the legend too.

Peter Fleischmann heard Warschauer boasting about having a famous wife from a wealthy Berlin family named Elisabeth Koshen. Fleischmann scoffed at the story because Koshen was his aunt and, as far as he knew, she remained single and in Germany. Of course, Warschauer was actually telling the truth, for once, and occasional victories like this only fueled the speculation about him. Meanwhile, he used every available opportunity to boost his own pedigree and laud his unique contribution to life in the square. Witness his essay for *The Camp Almanac*, published in Christmas, 1940.

"What has the school achieved?" he wrote. "Of the 170 pupils, many have been released, some dropped out, but in the great majority, love for technical matters and understanding for serious work has been roused.

Many have thanked us already, and many will thank us for opening to them a new possibility for a future profession. But we have achieved more. . . . The Technical School of Hutchinson Camp has furnished proof that under conscientious leadership and with the will fully aware of its aims, it is possible, in a comparatively short time, to give people a technical training of at least average standard; it has hereby proved that a big percentage of the refugees can be enabled to fulfil their one and greatest desire: to help England, and to become useful members of the economic machine of this country."

Those last lines read like a preemptive plea on his own behalf—that he be sent from the camp and back into society. The society into which he had come on Nazi business just over a year earlier.

Because of this fact, gaining release was going to prove harder for him than for all the others.

CHAPTER TEN

If Music Be the Food of Love

*Pleasanter and more important for the morale of the internees was
the highly respectable musical life. It was moving when fifty unhappy
men gathered in one of the narrow shabby rooms and listened to Professor Glas playing Bach, Mozart, or Schubert on a worn-out piano,
or to Rawicz's masterly melancholy jazz improvisations.*

—PROFESSOR PAUL JACOBSTHAL

EARLY IN 1935, THE PRINCE OF WALES WAS VISITING VIENNA WITH
Wallis Simpson. During a reception at the British Embassy on Jaures-
gasse, his ear was taken by a piano duo playing for the guests. Their names
were Walter Landauer and Maryan Rawicz, and the future King Edward
VIII was so impressed by their performance that afterward he sought
them out. The prince wanted them to know that their type of act would
be hugely popular in the music halls of England, and that they should
really consider trying their luck in London.

By November that year, Eric Maschwitz had engaged Rawicz and
Landauer to perform on his BBC radio show, *In Town Tonight*, their
first appearance presaged by a newspaper preview that described them
as accomplished Viennese pianists whose "selection of music is catholic;
both classical and popular pieces being included, and one of their spe-
cialties is Viennese waltzes." From that point until well into 1940, they
became regulars on the national broadcaster, and a staple on the nation-
wide touring circuit.

The prince's hunch had, indeed, been correct. There was a huge appetite in Britain for the double act of Rawicz and Landauer. An advertisement for their star turn at a National Sunday League concert at the Palladium invited fans to "a recital of compositions by Johann Strauss, Dvorak, Liszt, Kreisler, Tchaikovsky, and Weber, arranged for two pianofortes." One critic noted that everywhere they played they drew enormous applause, even though, unlike their contemporary competitors, they never bothered working current popular tunes into the act.

They were a curious pair. Rawicz was born in what was then Russian Poland, and studied law at the University of Krakow before moving to Vienna to pursue a career in music. Landauer had been born and reared in the Austrian capital where, soon after his own studies ended, he became a fixture on the local airwaves. Their professional relationship supposedly began by chance. At a resort hotel in 1929, Landauer heard Rawicz whistling a polka and asked him what it was. The ensuing conversation spawned a partnership that lasted until the Pole's death in 1970.

After decamping to England, the duo very quickly became stalwarts of the British entertainment establishment, even giving afternoon recitals in Harrods. Inevitably, their celebrity crossed over into movies, too. They played themselves in two films made in London, *The Street Singer* (1937) and *The Sky's the Limit* (1938). When war broke out one year after the release of the latter production, they immediately offered to help the only way they could. By one estimate, they played eighty Red Cross fundraisers during the first year of the conflict, concerts that yielded an estimated £30,000 (a sum worth around $2.8 million today) for the charity. They didn't forget their fellow Jews left behind in Vienna either, those who remained so vulnerable to Hitler.

"In 1937, when I was thirteen years old, I attended the wedding of my second cousin, Annie Wiesel, to Bertold Landauer, the brother of Walter Landauer," wrote Annette Saville. "The Rawicz and Landauer duo were sitting back-to-back at two pianos, on a specially constructed piano stool. They were already well established, earning lots of money and lifelong friends. In March 1938 Hitler's troops marched into Austria.

"Annie was very lucky indeed. Walter Landauer helped no fewer than six people to come to the UK—Annie and her husband, Annie's parents, and his own parents. He guaranteed their upkeep and had to give so much money to the government that his bank account was cleared out (though he soon recouped the money). He installed Annie and her husband in a flat in Streatham, in south London."

Philanthropy aside, Rawicz and Landauer also contributed to the war effort by performing on Armed Forces radio. Even while categorized as Category C aliens by a tribunal, they continued to work and to tour after the war had started. As late as June 22, 1940, they participated in a show on BBC radio, their last appearance on the wireless for some time. Soon after, the pair became yet another casualty of Churchill's "Collar the lot!" and, like émigré brethren around the country, were on their way to internment. They both ended up on the Isle of Man, albeit in different camps, and the injustice of their confinement even caused debate in national newspapers.

"I know that they consider England to be their home," wrote Walter Rowbottom, a friend of theirs, in a letter to *The Guardian*. "Since the outbreak of war, they have thrown their whole heart into the support of charitable causes, having given concerts and performances. . . . Because of their love of England and their whole-hearted support for our cause—'our common cause,' as they put it—they have refused many offers to go to the United States since the outbreak of war, and now they suffer for their love of our people and their support of our cause. If ever there was a clear case of wrongful detention, this is one."

It is a measure of the level of fame they had attained in Britain that Rawicz was recognized by Commander Daniel very early on in his time at Hutchinson. Constantly competitive about the status of his camp compared to others on the island, such as Onchan, Daniel recognized the presence of a celebrated pianist as an opportunity to score publicity points. His idea was simple enough—to reunite the famous interned duo for one night only, on his watch, with officers from all across the island invited. Rawicz was fine with the proposal when it was put to him. Landauer had no objection either.

Several houses in the square boasted a piano of some sort, and Rawicz tried them all, one even falling apart during his rather strenuous road test. Daniel knew that, for his special event, the star duo couldn't work with the inferior equipment that the landladies had kept for entertaining guests during peacetime. Somehow, from somewhere, the commander organized the rental and delivery of two Steinway Baby Grands. Only the finest instruments for the finest players. While Rawicz played for the residents of Hutchinson almost every evening until his release in mid-October, this dual performance alongside his erstwhile partner sums up the unique cultural life of the camp.

"I can still picture a lovely summer's afternoon on the crowded square, the internees crouching on the lawn, the officers and their ladies sitting on chairs in front of them, and the sentimental strains of Strauss, father and son, beautifully coaxed from the second-rate grand pianos by these two maestros, wafting across the distant sea," wrote Ronald Stent. "It was one of the highlights of the camp sojourn."

For the inmates, having a duo capable of selling out box offices all over Europe playing in the open air was indeed a boon, transporting them for the duration far beyond the barbed wire behind which they now lived. That sort of magical event put an end to an internal debate that had ensued about whether residents should devote every hour to resisting the authorities rather than amusing themselves with arts and entertainment. The argument was that, rather than enjoying music and theater or taking classes, their time might be better spent highlighting the stupidity of the policy of interning so many men who had fled the very regime Britain was fighting.

"Several inmates of the camp do not want to be entertained," wrote an unnamed correspondent in the sixth issue of *The Camp*, dated October 27, 1940. "They are afraid that a smile on their lips might affect their release. Some sophisticated ones say they do not need it; various events in Camp life, they argue, amuse them much more than any performance in the Palladium or Old Vic could do. There are a great many, however, who want some entertainment until they may leave Hutchinson Camp. What is being done for them?"

Plenty was being done for them. The musical agenda was structured, varied, and eagerly anticipated. The lineup for a concert on a September Sunday included Fritz Solomonski, an artist of some note, and Professor William`Cohn, an art historian, singing arias from Mozart's *The*

Marriage of Figaro; Professor Richard Glas playing Mozart and Chopin sonatas; and a Mr. Meyer delivering a Mozart flute concerto. Such was the demand for these events that a notice advised that those who didn't manage to get tickets for the initial show would be afforded the opportunity to see it again in a repeat performance the following Wednesday. There was also an advertisement about a chamber music recital set for Monday at 3:00 p.m., and a promise that this too would become a regular event on the calendar.

Professor Rudolf Kastner is credited with starting the chamber orchestra in the camp. Born in Vienna, he was formerly a critic with *Vossische Zeitung*, a liberal publication in Berlin, and *Münchner Neueste Nachrichten*, Munich's leading newspaper. A major figure in the vibrant musical culture of Weimar Germany, when he first suggested the idea to the camp commander, something was lost in translation, as Daniel believed they were looking to start a brass band. Once the difference was explained, however, he made good on a promise to secure instruments.

The sixty-one-year-old Kastner was a huge influence on the musical life of Hutchinson, even though his stay there was relatively brief. Some dilettantes did not enjoy his overlong introductions to the performances, believing he went into too much pedantic detail about the biography of every composer and the genesis of each work. But, upon his release in September, he assured those left behind that he'd send instruments and more sheet music the first chance he got. His was a magnanimous contribution.

"Under the leadership of Mr. Kastner, concerts were started," wrote Mr. Perlman in *The Camp*. "Later, particularly under Mr. Sluzewski's leadership, the weekly concert became a practice. Often, the overwhelming attendance made it necessary to repeat concerts several times. And, in addition to that, a small guild of music lovers assembled around the musicians and listened to a preliminary concert. Many will have had the same experience as I had: one was not satisfied with listening once, but tried to obtain a ticket for the repetition. It very much reminded me of the rehearsals at the Leipzig Gewandhaus, and we again saw how a group of music lovers formed itself amongst strangers under the influence of music."

The caliber of musical fare on offer can be gleaned from the formal bill printed to promote a concert on Thursday, November 7, 1940. According to the advertisement, it was "by invitation of the Commander of Hutchinson Camp, Douglas, Captain H. O. Daniel," and works by Handel, J. S. Bach, and Beethoven were to be performed by Curt Sluzewski on violin, and Professor Richard Glas and Hans Furth on pianos. Again, that trio of players captures the quality of musicians and the unique stories each brought with them to that tiny stage.

Sluzewski was perhaps the most enthusiastic yet least accomplished musician of the group. A veteran of World War I, where he had fought with the German army on the Russian front, and a distinguished lawyer by trade, the violin was his true passion. He played in a string quartet in his native Berlin and had a prominent role in establishing the city's Philharmonic Choir before the rise of Hitler and anti-Semitism brought the realization that he needed to get himself and his family to safety. "I must have water between me and that man," said Sluzewski.

In 1936, he moved to North West London and began working as a lawyer specializing in international legal matters. To understand his love of the violin, it's necessary to know that after the war, Sluzewski often paid professional musicians to visit his home to play with him on Sunday afternoons. Given the depth of his passion, the opportunity to rehearse and to perform, albeit in a prison camp, was at least to him something of a gift. He even kept a notebook lovingly recording details of every single concert during the course of his internment. And, somehow, he had his favorite instrument delivered to the Isle of Man.

If Sluzewski succeeded Kastner as the de facto spiritual leader of the musical community, Glas brought a better pedigree. Like so many others at Hutchinson, he too had seen his own promising career truncated by political events. A native of Austria, he studied under the great Leopold Godowsky at the Vienna Academy of Music, and in 1908 won a prestigious prize, a Bösendorfer grand piano, at the Vienna Conservatory. The knock on Glas was that while he was a supremely skilled musician, his playing deteriorated somewhat under pressure. This profile led, perhaps inevitably, to a teaching career that was going well until, of course, Hitler's annexation of Austria in 1938 meant his Jewishness cost him the job and forced him into exile in England. At Hutchinson, Glas discovered an audience for his music, quickly building a huge and devoted following among internees who savored the quality of his playing, even on the boardinghouse pianos deemed too inferior for Rawicz and Landauer.

"For one hour and in one room, there is no war," wrote a correspondent called Medicus in the fourth issue of *The Camp*. "The thrill and charm of beautiful music has banished it. Everybody was happy, and included in everybody was Professor Glas, the gifted pianist. A piano appears to me as an instrument in which extremes meet, the very name piano, soft, and forte, loud, are extremes, but between these our artists gave us a hundred variations of tone, the keys are black and white—again extremes—but the delightful shades of colour we heard were like listening to the song of birds or the laughter of children.

"Prof. Glas danced with his hands—making his own music to dance to, his hand would first meet then separate—then bow to each other and meet again, his nimble fingers rippling over the key-board. . . . The remarkable silence during this wonderful performance was only equalled by the tremendous applause which greeted the professor at the close. Thanks a thousand times, Professor. You have enriched the lives of all who heard you and given us a happy memory which we will all cherish."

Glas took it upon himself to pass on his wealth of knowledge to Furth, a precocious twenty-year-old whose journey to the Isle of Man had been typically peripatetic. Many thought he was even younger than that because there was something of the boy wonder about an individual who had been showing immense musical promise since the age of five.

Born into a Jewish family in Vienna, the only child to ever show interest in the house piano, Furth was soon good enough to be accepted into the city's storied conservatory for advanced lessons, even though the family couldn't afford to pay the required fees. By his early teens, he was giving public recitals, his progress onto the concert stage all the more remarkable because the Furth household didn't boast a radio or a gramophone. The first time he heard a symphony by Bach or Beethoven was when he played it himself.

As his nascent music career was blossoming, Furth's other great passion was the Boy Scouts, an organization that taught him and many of his teenage peers in 1930s Austria the virtues of self-sufficiency, a skill some of them needed to survive when forced to leave after the arrival of the Nazis. The Furths were not religious and had no objections when Hans was baptized Catholic at the age of sixteen, a conversion that was still not enough to spare him once Hitler's emissaries were on the prowl.

Shortly after his own conversion, his by then divorced mother married an elderly Yugoslav Jew in order to secure a passport for that country. That was her ticket out of an Austria undergoing full Nazification, a place where any semblance of Jewishness was going to spell doom for people. Half of her family ended up being killed in the Holocaust. In August of 1938 Furth followed his mother to what would today be called Croatia, and after a spell living just outside Zagreb, ended up trekking back across Europe. Bound for Zurich, he jumped the train at Antwerp, and, from there, eventually secured a visa for England.

Originally allowed into the country to train as a farmer before being shipped off to work in Australia as part of a YMCA scheme, Furth's musical talent led, instead, to him being recategorized. Instead of learning how to tend animals and crops, he had a sojourn living with an organist in St. Ives near Cornwall.

"This is where I was when the war started," said Furth. "I made some friends, gave a little concert, got some money together, but really didn't know what I was going to do. There wasn't much future. This was when the war started. I was in Cornwall, my mother was in London; she came to Cornwall when the Blitzkrieg started. My mother got a job working as a maid down there, then the bombing stopped, and she went back. Eventually, I decided to go back. I got back to London, and got a scholarship to the Royal Academy of Music."

After a few months, he received a certificate from the academy, a feat that unfortunately coincided with the rounding up of German and Austrian refugees. There were so many men to be picked up in London that Furth and many others realized, at least for a time, they could avoid internment with the minimum of effort.

"If you got out of your house by seven in the morning, you were saved," said Furth. "They usually came between seven and eight in the morning, so if you were out of the house by then you were safe. So, my piano teacher told me to come for breakfast every morning at half past six. After some time I got tired and said, 'Why shouldn't the King look after me?' There was a note left by the police: 'Will you please stay in so we can get you?' Very polite, so I stayed in and they got me. Eventually I was sent to the Isle of Man."

As a young man who'd spent the previous two years evading Hitler's clutches and trying to find a home, Furth didn't regard being billeted in a camp teeming with so many brilliant minds, of every different stripe, as that much of a punishment. Younger and fitter than most inmates, he did not have as much to worry about, leaving no wife or children or career behind. Instead, he arrived at Hutchinson blessed with musical ability, something that guaranteed he also had a fulfilling way of passing the time.

"This was the highlight of my musical career," said Furth. "I was surrounded by scientists of all kinds, surrounded by musicians of all kinds. For the first time, I played chamber music. You had some violin players, and I was one of the only good pianists, so I was very much in demand. And we gave so many concerts. I also met a brilliant pianist who gave me piano lessons, Glas. I really had a great time and had no intention of leaving until eventually people left. We were treated wonderfully. We made music, I studied the piano; it was like a university, make music and study, and arrange concerts and attend lectures."

For Furth, the budding concert pianist, much like for the enthusiastic amateur Sluzewski, Hutchinson represented a chance to practice and play in an environment where so many of the other men were thrilled by the soundtrack they provided. As the first summer segued into autumn and the realization hit that many of them might be spending the winter behind barbed wire, music was an important release, a daily distraction, wondrous notes reminding them that the world at war was still capable of producing something so beautiful.

"I like to recall some picturesque performances, for instance, a concert in front of the houses of the front row, when some were hanging out of the windows as in Italian operas, while the musicians played and sang on the front steps with the crowded audience in front of them on the lawns and right down the pavement, fascinating even outsiders beyond the wire," wrote Mr. Perlman. "Or Mr. Glas playing Beethoven sonatas in the dining room of a house, drawing by the magic of his play innumerable persons into the room, waiting outside to listen through the window and waiting for the repetition. Or a night in the hall when the room had an intriguing atmosphere of its own, with the pictures and sculptures arranged for an exhibition.

"In spite of a continual lack of musical material and particularly in spite of most inadequate instruments, which were hardly pianos, we heard some wonderful performances of Beethoven, Mozart, Schubert, etc. . . . . And whereas it was Glas and Furth who played us pieces of classical music, it was Maryan Rawicz who revived Viennese waltzes and whose playing of Jazz including his own compositions cheered everybody up. We older listeners to music hall had particular pleasure, finding all our favorite works performed in these strange circumstances, but the young ones too found pleasure in the discovery of great music, helping all of us over our present hardships."

Aside from weekly concerts, there were other outlets for music as well. The camp's Youth Group invited Glas and Dr. Egon Wellesz, along with Furth, to provide an evening of high culture to the younger inmates, some of whom might not have been exposed to classical music by that point in their lives. Before Glas and Furth started the evening with a sonata by Mozart for four hands, Wellesz offered the audience a primer in what they were about to hear, a quick lesson so they might better appreciate the quality of the fare on offer. They must have been fast learners, because the double act held them in thrall.

"During these recitals an extraordinary silence prevailed, such as [had] not happened before," wrote one member of the Youth Group. "The light of the candles and the strange room helped to establish a perfect atmosphere for the concert. The performance of such wonderful music so perfectly played held us to such an extent as we have not yet experienced during our internment. We are grateful to all artists who had given their help. . . . It was for many of us a first introduction to classical music; our approach to it will now be easier, as we may have learnt to appreciate it."

The members of the Youth Group were no slouches either. Even before organizing that particular evening of top-class entertainment, they had been attracting packed houses to weekly get-togethers they billed as *bunter abend* (social evenings). Such was the popularity of a choir they started that they expanded to incorporate a singing section, so those perhaps too intimidated to sing formally could still come along and belt out familiar, more popular tunes in a safe space.

All that was good about the cultural life of the camp is exemplified by the interaction between the Youth Group and Messrs. Glas, Furth, and Wellesz. By virtue of being confined together, this bunch of enthusiastic neophytes gained quick and fruitful access, not just to stellar performers, but also to the immense knowledge of Wellesz. Most of those sitting in the room listening to his preamble before the concert probably didn't know or appreciate that this helpful introduction was being delivered by one of the foremost musicologists in Europe, maybe even the world. Witness the fulsome prose with which the *Oxford Magazine* greeted his appointment to a three-year fellowship at Lincoln College back in January, 1939.

"We congratulate Lincoln College on the election of Dr. Egon Wellesz, late Professor of Music at the University of Vienna, to a Research Fellowship in Byzantine Music. We congratulate Oxford on the acquisition of so eminent a scholar, composer and historian. Dr. Wellesz is not only the great authority on the history of Byzantine music, but also on the history of opera. . . . As a distinguished composer of the modern Vienna school, he brings with him to Oxford views on its music, and those who make it, which will be of great interest. They will be helpful and always welcomed, sometimes even provoking."

That encomium neglected to mention that the new job came at the end of several years of uncertainty and strife during which Wellesz's academic and musical pedigree counted for less and less because he had been born Jewish. Although he later converted to Roman Catholicism, the religion of his birth cost him what had been an exalted place in the Austrian musical firmament in the 1920s and 1930s. Even before the arrival of Hitler's troops in the country, the rising tide of anti-Semitism effectively ended what had been a stellar career on a number of fronts.

"As a composer, musicologist, teacher and organizer," wrote Hans Redlich, "Egon Wellesz is one of the most striking representatives of the old land of culture that was Austria."

In that land of culture, he had studied under the great Arnold Schoenberg (about whom he later wrote a biography), completed a doctorate on the Austro-Italian composer Giuseppe Bonno, and joined the staff at the University of Vienna in 1913. Rising to the position of professor of music, Wellesz earned international renown for his important investigations of Byzantine music, somehow juggling those academic pursuits with finding his own voice as a composer. He wrote ballets, operas, and even liturgical works for the church, and his reputation stretched all the way to England.

"In February 1932, Hugh Allen, the then Heather Professor of Music at Oxford, wrote to Wellesz . . . that an honorary doctorate of music would be bestowed on him in recognition of his achievements as a composer and a scholar," wrote Bojan Bujic, "and to mark the occasion of the second centenary of the birth of Joseph Haydn, the only previous holder of an Oxford DMus to have hailed from Austria."

If that kind of accolade spoke to his stature in music, it counted for little as the decade wore on. Performances of his works were eventually prohibited because of his Jewish background. The fact he had become a devout Catholic counted for naught. He was fortunate to be in Amsterdam for a performance of *Prospero's Entreaties*, his three-movement symphonic poem for large orchestra, when news came through of the Anschluss. Rather than return to Vienna, Wellesz exploited his excellent connections in England's music community to move to London.

Harry Colles, music critic for *The Times*, introduced him to George Dyson, who then invited him to address his students at the Royal College of Music, an opportunity that helped make the case he was somebody with specialist knowledge, a detail he felt was key in helping him to stay in Britain.

"These lectures," wrote Wellesz, "made it possible for me to remain in England and not to fall into the hands of the Gestapo, who held at that time my wife and daughter as hostages."

His wife, Dr. Emmy Stross, and their daughter Elisabeth were eventually released and able to join him in Oxford, but the reunion was cut short by his arrest and internment at Hutchinson. While Furth enjoyed the routine of camp life and Sluzewski relished the opportunity to play music each day, internment had a deleterious impact on Wellesz. He didn't compose a single note between 1938 and 1944, and, although in one early letter to his wife, he described the camp as something of a spa for men, being imprisoned took an enormous psychological toll, leading to an eventual breakdown.

Many of the residents battled anxiety about where they were headed next and how long they would be incarcerated, so Wellesz was not alone in battling depression and mental health issues. Hellmuth Weissenborn recalled that he vented his own emotional anger by shouting and swearing like never before. One resident feigned symptoms of illness in order to spend most of his stay at the camp hospital. Another flung himself repeatedly against the barbed wire until his cuts required medical attention. One more suffered ghastly hallucinations about being murdered by his fellow residents and was eventually transferred to an asylum.

Wellesz's struggles stand in marked contrast to the experience of Furth, his younger musical collaborator, who enjoyed life in the camp so much that he never bothered applying for release, even as that was often uppermost in the minds of those around him. In the end, after nine months in captivity, his lack of interest in getting out prompted a call for him to report to the office.

"What are you still doing here?" asked Commander Daniel.

"Sir, I don't fall into any of the rubrics [laid out in the various government White Papers categorizing those eligible for release]," replied Furth.

"What do you mean, you don't fall into any of the rubrics. You are an excellent pianist!"

Daniel produced a copy of the White Paper and pointed out the relevant section, which dictated that any world-famous musician, artist, or writer, whose status was endorsed by an outside institution, would be free to go.

"I'm not world famous!" protested Furth.

"You can say that you hope to be!" said Daniel.

Duly motivated, Furth put in his first formal request to be released, citing his exceptional musical ability and intention to one day be world famous. That might not have been enough to swing it, but Ralph Vaughan Williams, the famous English composer and chair of the Home Office Committee for the Release of Interned Alien Musicians, was so impressed by the caliber of men he'd been playing with in the camp that he signed off on the boy wonder's release.

CHAPTER ELEVEN

The Writing on the Wall

The human being is not content to live and vegetate only. The ten-
dency to produce, to create and to build up whatever it may be is
deeper rooted in our conscience than many of us believe. To keep this
spirit even under the most difficult circumstances, not to loose [sic]
heart under hard conditions and to secure progress wherever we are
is more than our duty—it is our fate. We all know the situation here.
Yet, we see that today, after exactly four months in this camp, the
Spirit is unbroken, nay, stronger than before. There is a difference
between strain and concentration. Undoubtedly, some in our midst
feel nothing but the strain in being interned and isolated; the others,
however, have been able to concentrate, to [be]come stronger in their
personalities—and to create.

    —MICHAEL CORVIN, "LIFE, ART AND FUTURE," *THE CAMP,*
NOVEMBER 13, 1940

HEINRICH FRAENKEL WALKED INTO COMMANDER DANIEL'S OFFICE
with a little more assurance and confidence than most. He'd been here
before. During what most residents of Hutchinson described as "the first
war," Fraenkel had also been a guest of the state on the Isle of Man. Not
yet seventeen at the outbreak of that conflict, an innocent schoolboy
visiting England had been swept up in the hysteria and imprisoned at
sprawling Knockaloe Internment Camp, just eleven miles to the west on

the other side of the island, a place where twenty-four thousand Germans, Austrians, and Turks were held for the duration.

At Knockaloe, Fraenkel made the best of a bad situation. Far from home in a country now hostile to his own, he treated the camp as a type of finishing school. Under the tutelage of a Professor Albers, he completed his studies for the *Abitur* (the certificate marking the end of secondary education in Germany). He also used his time behind barbed wire to become almost fluent in English and to turn himself into a formidable chess player, two skills that would serve him well for the rest of his life.

He stood before Daniel then as no greenhorn but as somebody experienced in the ways of internment, and a man carrying a rather bizarre set of requests. In a place where every inmate had a complaint about facilities and the lack of various necessities, Fraenkel recited a list of requirements that included a small private room to write in, a typewriter, and a specific set of books, documents, and papers to be transported to the Isle of Man forthwith. He needed this and more if he were to submit the manuscript of his latest book to Victor Gollancz in London on time.

"What is your book called?" asked Daniel.

"*Help Us Germans to Beat the Nazis!*" replied Fraenkel.

Despite the shortage of living space in the overcrowded camp, a nook was found for him to write, a typewriter sourced for him to use, and, eventually, his research notes too were delivered. Which meant, just weeks after being arrested as a potential enemy alien, forty-two-year-old Fraenkel knuckled down to the task of completing a manifesto designed to help the British authorities and people understand how they might defeat Hitler and his movement—while in custody behind barbed wire at the behest of the British government.

"It so happens that while writing this book I have to stay behind barbed wire in a British internment camp," wrote Fraenkel, opening his epilogue. "It may seem strange, but I really could not think of a better place to write this book—none more suitable, anyway. As I look out at the pleasant background of Douglas town and bay (with barbed wire looming prominently in the foreground), I am surrounded by a teeming crowd of fellow internees, most of whom are restlessly pacing up and down the grounds or round and round the barbed-wire borders of our little realm. That crowd is a most instructive one for any student of contemporary German history; it is a crowd that, with certain modifications, may well be considered a cross section of the German people."

It is not clear whether the curious subject matter of the book or Fraenkel's pedigree as a writer convinced Daniel to give him preferential treatment. Certainly, the way his demands were met was in marked contrast to the artists and sculptors initially working with found material they had scavenged around the camp. By this point in his career, Fraenkel had put together an impressive résumé as a journalist, author, and screenwriter. Having been to Hollywood to write for Metro-Goldwyn-Mayer and Warner Bros., his film credits, in the United States and Britain, included work alongside directors of the caliber of Wilhelm Dieterle and actors like Boris Karloff and Joan Wyndham.

If that sounds like a fairly glamorous transatlantic life—indeed, he gave a lecture to the camp on the workings of Hollywood one December night—Fraenkel had also fit in his share of politics, too. During a brief return to Germany, he'd discovered himself wanted by the Nazis in the frenzied aftermath of the Reichstag Fire in 1933, and before ending up back in London toward the end of the decade, he also fought fascism in the Spanish Civil War. Somewhere, among all that, he had married Gretel Levy-Ries (no relation to Klaus Hinrichsen's wife, with whom she shared much of her name). He'd already packed a whole lot into his forty-two years. And he wasn't done fighting, or writing.

Angered by one of the local newspapers in the Isle of Man describing the internees as "the Huns," Fraenkel wrote a column for *The Camp*, pointing out the ignorance involved in using that term.

"Since it so happens that the book I am writing deals with our native opposition against the Nazis and with the better Germany and Europe," he wrote, "which, one day, we all hope to be part of (and which so many of us have struggled and bled for), may I take this opportunity of voicing a similar problem which I know we all have very much at heart: the recent attacks against us in the local press.

"When the editors call us 'Huns'—us, not the depraved Hitler-serfs who are bombing women and children—when letters to the editors complain that, having robbed the Manx people of their homes, we shouldn't rob them of their self-respect too, we may commiserate with the first part of the latter statement, but we certainly owe it to our own self-respect to protest most emphatically with those who are our own arch-enemies; after all, there are many of us who have been suffering hell in Himmler's concentration camps, and quite a few of us who, at home and in exile, have been fighting Hitlerism tooth and nail; indeed we may well say that we have been at it with Hitler for more than six years before this country came in."

Cleverly, he ended the piece by pointing out that most right-thinking people knew the true character of those in the internments camps, a fact he believed was most evident in the "tact" and "courtesy" evinced by the officers at Hutchinson toward the inmates. Perhaps this was best illustrated by how Daniel had treated him and his request for assistance.

Hours after police in a Black Maria had picked up Richard Friedenthal at his house in Hampstead, the forty-four-year-old arrived at the desk processing new arrivals in the temporary camp at Kempton Park Racecourse. In one hand, he carried a suitcase full of clothes; in the other, he clutched his beloved typewriter. A kerfuffle when he was being taken into custody—a German-American neighbor was being wrongly arrested—allowed him to smuggle the typewriter into the vehicle without the officers seeing it. Now, he stood across the table from a Buckingham Guard, worried he might lose his prized possession.

"What is your profession?" asked the soldier, with the tone of somebody who felt, like many of his colleagues, that this bureaucratic drudge work was not what they had signed up for.

"A writer," replied Friedenthal.

"A writer? What do you mean by a writer?"

"I'm writing books. I'm an author." He punctuated the sentence by reaching into his case and pulling out the wraparound cover of *The White Gods*, his fictional account of Hernando Cortes conquering Mexico, which had been published in London by Heinemann.

"Aha," said the soldier, now understanding what he meant. "Keeps you busy, eh?"

The soldier had been so intrigued by Friedenthal's exotic occupation and dazzled perhaps by the book jacket that he didn't notice the typewriter under his armpit. The machine stayed in his grasp through the night he spent sleeping on the floor of the betting hall at Kempton Park and over the course of a subsequent month at a camp in Prees Heath in Shropshire. It remained with him all the way to Hutchinson, and when word got around the square about what the new arrival had managed to bring with him, strangers began knocking on his door, asking for help typing up their applications for release.

Most of them didn't know or care about the fact that Friedenthal had edited the world's first compact German-language encyclopedia, *Konversationslexikon*, nearly a decade earlier. They just knew he had the tools and the ability to type a letter that might help them get out of the camp and back to their families. So, while Fraenkel holed up in his garret, trying to finish a manuscript he had grand notions could contribute to the defeat of Hitler, Friedenthal spent chunks of his time learning the life stories of many of the men in his midst.

His own tale was typical. From a Protestant family, where his father's people were originally Jewish, he served as a decorated lieutenant in the German army in World War I, where he was wounded at Verdun. His military service and the fact that the Friedenthals' Jewishness was historic rather than current had kept him somewhat protected from the Nazi menace, although he was prevented from publishing new work after 1933. At the end of 1938, he finally abandoned his career as director of a Berlin publishing house, fleeing to London under the pretense of needing to do six weeks of research at the British Museum. He arrived with just ten reichsmarks in his pocket.

Men coming to him at Hutchinson, seeking his assistance and typing skills, had even stranger yarns to unspool. Like the elderly Jewish man who'd arrived in the East End of London in 1895, built up a prosperous carpentry shop, and put together a property portfolio, without ever becoming naturalized—an oversight that caused his internment after nearly half a century as an upstanding member of English society.

"What kind of reference have you got?" asked Friedenthal as he sat at the typewriter.

"Put down Herbert Morrison," answered his new best friend.

Morrison was, first, minister of supply and, later, home secretary, in Churchill's War Cabinet, a title that meant he was overseeing the entire internment process.

"What have you to do with Herbert Morrison?" enquired Friedenthal, thinking the attempt to involve a high-ranking politician in the release application a tad far-fetched.

"Well, Herbert Morrison will remember me very well because when he was standing for his first election as a councillor, I organized the Jewish vote for him," replied the man, laughing.

Friedenthal advised his friend that it might be better to have his wife and family write directly to Morrison. A piece of counsel that resulted weeks later in Commander Daniel calling Friedenthal into the office and showing him a letter which the minister had written to the spouse to advise her he couldn't do anything for her husband. Daniel seemed incredulous that the politician responsible for internment had written personally to the woman, at least until Friedenthal explained the circumstances.

In his role as unofficial camp typist, Friedenthal learned the intimate details of the lives and passions of his fellow internees. He also threw himself into the lecturing circuit at Hutchinson, speaking on topics like Leonardo da Vinci, Haydn, the contrasts between England and America in the eighteenth century, and the nature of the Elizabethan theater. Before delivering a class on William Shakespeare, he commissioned a carpenter housemate to construct a wooden model of the Globe Theatre so he could use it as a teaching prop in the classroom, to better explain the geography of the stage.

Between typing up letters for his peers and lecturing, Friedenthal still found time to try to effect his own release. In this regard, he wrote letters to the PEN Club and to Stefan Zweig, the celebrated Austrian novelist who was such a good friend he'd given Friedenthal a place to stay when he'd first arrived in London. By 1940 Zweig was touring South America, but had not forgotten the plight of his pal.

"He was at a party given by the foreign ministry in Buenos Aires and the foreign minister asked him, 'Now, Mr. Zweig, is there anything I can do you for you?' He said, very kindly, 'You could do me a great favour if you sent a visa for my friend Friedenthal who is at present interned in the Isle of Man, that he should then come to Argentina.' Within a week the minister had sent a cable to the Argentine embassy in London saying there was a visa for Dr. Friedenthal. This was then transmitted to the camp."

It all happened so fast that people around the square were already coming up to Friedenthal, congratulating him on his imminent departure. They hadn't taken into account the bureaucratic red tape still to be navigated. The Argentine ambassador in London decided he could only issue a visa to somebody who turned up at the embassy in person. Commander Daniel took the view that no prisoner could leave Hutchinson without first showing him a valid visa for going to another country. The situation could not be resolved, so Friedenthal remained where he was.

Under the circumstances, it wasn't the worst place in the world to be, especially for a novelist, for whom access to this vast cross section of society was eventually to prove manna from creative heaven. Friedenthal also felt his own military experience made it easier for him to cope with life in such a rigid environment—that, and the pleasure of taking it all in.

"It was teeming mankind," said Friedenthal. "The experience itself was total life. What interested me most was the growing up of a community under very special conditions, growing up and developing at the same time as it has been in history with the various tribes. So, there were strongly developed tribal jealousies, pride, and leadership. Tribal leaders, after a time, appeared in the various places, and later on party life, cultural life, in the various stages from rather primitive to the most refined conditions of Dadaism and ironic refinery."

More than a decade later, he distilled that view into a novel called *Die Welt in der Nussschale* (The World in a Nutshell), based upon his experiences at Hutchinson, the inevitable consequence of what he'd been through. Names were changed to protect the reputations of those involved and certain characters were merged together in his retelling, but any internee who chose to read it (it was never published in English) could easily recognize the individuals portrayed.

"I was very often asked 'Who is that? Who is that?'" he said. "Of course, in a good novel, the persons are a combination of various experiences. Sometimes if they just look and sound very realistic and typical, they are just composed of three or four different persons, perhaps with some added touch by the author. My main idea was to describe this and these people. In addition, I put in quite a lot of fun and humour because, in retrospect it didn't sound so terribly tragical to me; it was tragical enough at the time. We had quite a number of suicides, people getting mad and all that kind of thing."

Franz Boensch (aka, Frank Hartl) didn't wait so long to be creatively inspired by his surroundings. One of the driving forces behind the campaign to bring theater to the internees, the strange circumstances of his captivity compelled him to rewrite a play he felt had taken on much greater significance given where these men now found themselves—isolated, literally and metaphorically, on an island. He was the man behind the square's production of *The Good Soldier Schwejk*, a work cited by many internees as something that stuck with them long after they had left the Isle of Man.

Boensch knew more than most about the power of theater in strained circumstances. A native of Vienna, he lived in Berlin from 1929 to 1937, years during which he led a mendicant existence, cutting his teeth as an actor, writer, and activist alongside left-wing luminaries such as Erwin Piscator. A committed communist, Boensch was part of the avant-garde outfit, Sturmtrupp Alarm, and, later, a member of Truppe 1931, two agitprop companies renowned for using the stage as a venue for party political commentary and critiques of society. Having been imprisoned for his membership in the communist party once the Nazis took over, he eventually escaped to London in 1937.

There, he found an outlet for his energies in the Laterndl, a theater company which he founded alongside Fritz Schrecker and Franz Schultz. Their intention was to perform German-speaking drama to entertain the growing community of Austrian exiles around the city and to do the type of topical work capable of informing an English audience about the deteriorating conditions in their homeland. The opening night of their first production at the Austrian Centre in Paddington in June 1939, a series of nine short sketches called *Unterwegs* (On the Road), was attended by, among others, H. G. Wells and J. B. Priestley.

In the spring of 1940, the Laterndl, now based out of Finchley Road, put on *Der unsterbiche Schwejk* (The Immortal Schwejk), a reworking of the Czech writer Jaroslav Hasek's novel *The Good Soldier Schwejk*. Boensch and some of his colleagues rewrote or reimagined scenes from Hasek's post–World War I comic masterpiece about subverting authority, making it even more relevant in a Europe newly enmeshed in another conflict. The work was bold enough in its attack on the Nazis and Hitler to garner headlines and positive reviews in the London press.

Within weeks of those notices, Boensch was interned at Hutchinson, a small detail that didn't prevent him from continuing the work of producing the type of overtly political cabaret the Austrians called *Kleinkunst*. Where better than an internment camp full of enemies of Hitler to stage a piece in which Schwejk, the central figure, is a bumbling innocent who manages to expose the folly of the bureaucrats in charge? Boensch pieced together a series of twelve sketches, some inspired by his previous work with the Laterndl, more influenced by his new life behind barbed wire on the Isle of Man.

Given that the original novel had been burned by the Nazis, it was the perfect comic fodder for men who had escaped a fascist regime only to then be imprisoned in the country of their liberation. Exactly the type of unfortunate misadventure that befalls Schwejk, as he blunders around the Austro-Hungarian Empire, trying to be a good soldier but constantly getting undone by the vagaries of life. Hutchinson contained plenty of men who had fought Hitler at home for years only to find themselves imprisoned by those now fighting the same man in France.

"The last scene, 'Blackout in Prague, 1938,' written by Franz Boensch, closed the play most vivid[ly] and full of actuality," wrote Criticus in a review for *The Camp* on Tuesday, December 10, 1940. "It was also 'shwejky' and significant that the producer himself, F. Boensch, was not present at the first night, as he was released just the day before. *The Good Soldier Schwejk* was undoubtedly the best theatrical performance seen in this camp so far, and we hope to see the same 'Players' Guild' very soon with a new production."

Others were equally impressed by both the content and the performances.

"It was a daring enterprise to produce full-length plays in a simple lounge or dining room of a boardinghouse, without proper lighting, without any one of the expedients usually thought to be indispensable for a stage," wrote Michael Corvin. "But, it was done, and the success of *Of Mice and Men* and *The Good Soldier Schwejk* justified the producers and encouraged the actors rightly. At the shortest notice the mentioned players were rehearsed and [plays] produced and especially the brave *Schwejk*, which ran in a serial of five performances—was seen by practically everybody in the Camp."

Boensch and a troupe of players that included Otto Tausig, Gerry Wolff, Erwin Jacoby, Jochen Weigert, Perry Weiss, Philo Hauser, and Fritz Weiss proved adept at making the best of limited facilities and props to produce work so memorable that, more than half a century later, Freddy Godshaw offered this reminiscence to the BBC.

"Some events still stand out in my mind and I shall never forget them," he said. "A production of *Of Mice and Men*, the John Steinbeck play. It was performed in one of the bedrooms with no more than about twenty people packed in tight as an audience. But what an outstanding performance! Someone wrote a skit on a Shakespeare play but called it *Romeo and Julian*. It was hilarious. The theme was that they were gay."

While some older residents refused to acknowledge its very existence and others testified it was inconsequential, there seems to have been a clandestine gay scene in the camp. In a couple of rooms, some younger internees had pushed the mattresses together, and this was considered evidence they were in sexual relationships. In another incident, a minor kerfuffle ensued when an older gentleman from across the square was found en flagrante with an inmate many years his junior.

"We had only problems with the youngsters," said Fritz Hallgarten. "There was quite a lot of masturbation going on, and we learned a few had started homosexual practices with the result that we ourselves approached the commander and told him something had to be done. From that time, bromide was put in the food. There was guessing about in which food the bromide went. Did it go into the porridge? Did it go into the tea? There was some guessing and some betting but it was never found out; I think it was in the porridge."

Where there were playwrights and writers, there were also readers. Lots of them. Many struggling to access books in their new homes. The lack of reading material was a common complaint from internees in the opening weeks of their time in Hutchinson. In the very first issue of *The Camp*, a letter writer calling himself simply "Reader" had welcomed the arrival of the publication, but pointed out that a proper library was a much more pressing concern for him and his colleagues.

When it first opened, the library, if it could even be called that, consisted of a dusty room with a bare floor carpeted with mostly detective novels and thrillers. From such humble beginnings, it grew into a formidable institution that served the camp well, greatly helped by generous donations from bodies like the YMCA. Orange boxes from the canteen were commandeered and pressed into service for storage and later broken down to make shelves. And the campaign to get more tomes involved everybody with a vested interest.

Books were donated by the Oxford University Press, Victor Gollancz, and the British Council, loaned from the National Central and Douglas libraries, and purchased from the library fund. The taste in literature ran the gamut.

"Books by Freud, popular science books like Jeans' *Mysterious Universe*, Eddington, Julian Huxley are always asked for; so are well-known authors like H. G. Wells, Shaw, Galsworthy, English classics like *Alice in Wonderland*, so-called 'best-sellers' like Cronin's *Citadel* and Trevelyan, and of course books on the English language," reported *The Camp*. "Another type of books much in demand are books on Jewish History and Culture, e.g., the extremely well-produced *Legacy of Israel*, but also novels dealing with Jewish life, [like] *Mottke Der Dieb* by Schalom Asch and others. . . . We have only got [a] few German books, and not the very best imaginable; this is an additional reason for us to try and encourage our readers to read books written in English."

According to the librarians, 60 percent of internees used it at some point or other. Some of the men were also receiving packages of books from friends, although these were usually specific to their area of knowledge. Dr. Gunther Zuntz, for instance, whose last published work before arrest was an essay on "The Western Texts of the Acts of the Apostles," received parcels of books from C. C. Torrey, an Aramaic scholar and theologian, with whom he shared a research interest.

Because of the improvised nature of the facility and the haphazard supply chain, some internees found reason to complain.

"The present system adopted in our library gives cause for complaint," wrote a correspondent calling himself E. W. Sch in *The Camp*. "A lover of books likes to make his choice after handling and fondling the book he proposes to read. He loves to skim through the pages to see if there are any pictures; in short, he treats his objects like a lover treats a girl before he chooses. Your present system is cold and impersonal. The books have been given to us all by generous and kindhearted donors. They are meant to brighten the dark and sometimes unbearable hours of captivity. We should have the full benefit of these valuable presents, giving us an easy access to the books, time and space to pick and choose. Over-anxious officialdom and small-minded tactics should be ruled out as much as possible. Everybody should feel that the camp library is for the benefit and enjoyment of us all."

If the tomes destined for Zuntz were hardly likely to appeal to most inmates, the appetite for wider reading was such that by November, some men received permission for and organized a "Reading Room" where those willing to pay a membership fee could come and peruse a selection of international and British publications.

"Fellow internees, interested in politics, economics, social questions, literature or overseas development, and wanting information beyond that provided by the wireless and the Daily papers will be glad to learn that a Reading Room has been opened at House 35 (Silverside)," went the notice. "THE READING ROOM is open to subscribers only, the weekly subscription amounts to 6d, the hours are 10:00 a.m.–12:30 p.m., 2:30 p.m.–4:30 p.m." Only a small and unspecified number of gentlemen would be allowed to join, and "the committee reserves the right to close the list after this number has been reached."

The list of publications available was eclectic and impressive. It included *Canada's Weekly, Empire News, The Economist, The Statist, The*

New Statesman, Jewish Chronicle, Crown Colonist, Reader's Digest, Nineteenth Century, Spectator, Times Literary Supplement, Manchester Guardian Weekly, News Review, the *Illustrated London News, Picture Post, Saturday Evening Post, Life* magazine, and *Lilliput.*

Having warned the men that membership would be restricted, there came a sales pitch beneath the list of periodicals. Under the heading *Look Out into the World,* internees were warned to broaden their horizons and to start thinking internationally, educating themselves for the changes afoot all over the planet.

"Whereas Europe is entangled in a battle of destruction, the spirit of enterprise blossoms in other parts of the earth, which are twenty times larger than Europe. . . . Soon we may have to step into these vast areas of the world. Therefore, we should not confine our thoughts to the sensations of the day, but direct our attention to significant developments of the continents of Asia, Australia, Africa, and America. Every week we can read in certain Periodicals about districts, even the names of which were hardly known to us, now being the scene of rising industrial activities on an unbelievable scale, of new-to-me commercial centres, and settlements, cultural problems deriving therefrom."

The creation of such a space and the nature of the stock it carried bespoke a literate community with a wide range of interests and a keen eye on seismic events happening in the world beyond the barbed wire hemming them in at Hutchinson. Indeed, within two weeks of the Reading Room opening for business, one of the assistants wrote an article for *The Camp,* outlining how patrons, apparently oblivious to the fact they were behind barbed wire, could be rather demanding.

"It is a very interesting job," he wrote. "We start at 10 o'clock in the morning. A few minutes later came to me the first customer. He asked for the *Australian Times.* 'Sorry, Sir,' I told him. 'Of the daily papers we have *The Times* and the *Manchester Guardian.*' He was dissatisfied. Another gentleman asked for *The Humorist.* I offered him *Punch.* He prefers *The Humorist,* he said. A young clergyman took *The Contemporary Review* and *Nineteenth Century.* 'I will also glance over that,' he said. And I saw in his hands *London Opinion,* too. I must report he perused the latter and glanced only at the two serious magazines.

"Young people ask for *The Times, Trade and Engineering*, but prefer also *Picture Post, Illustrated London News* and the excellent *Life. The New Statesman* and *Nation, Time & Tide, Spectator* are very liked. One gentleman reads only *The Economist*, another *Saturday Evening Post*. Some of our readers saw by our institution for the first time *News Review* or *Cavalcade*. We have got a lot of Daily and Weekly Papers, Periodicals and Pamphlets. For 6d weekly, one can read them in House 35 (Silverside); will you join us? But don't ask for *Il Mundo* from Lisbon, like a fellow today."

CHAPTER TWELVE

The Art of War

Time marches on. War and peace take their turns in the life of nations. Generations are born, generations pass away—but art lasts. True works of art endure through all trials and tribulations of the age; they survive as eternal tokens of what was best in the generation that created them. What a strength of character, what indomitable vitality is shown by our artists here who in spite of all this pressure in their minds and souls preserve in fulfilling their mission on earth: to form and depict the beauty of nature and creation.
—SIEGFRIED OPPENHEIMER, *THE CAMP ALMANAC*,
DECEMBER 1940

THE FORTUNES OF THE ARTISTS BILLETED AT HUTCHINSON WERE greatly improved by a sporting event. Following the camp's defeat by nearby Onchan on the football field, Commander Daniel was dismayed. He took great pride in his being the preeminent facility on the island in every possible way, so losing the game irked him greatly. It also made him very receptive to a suggestion from Siegfried Oppenheimer, a loquacious art dealer in civilian life, that the quality of artists living in the square merited the holding of an exhibition to showcase their works.

"Oppenheimer was one of those somewhat over life-size characters, constantly quoting Goethe and addressing every other artist as Meister [Master], and liable to exaggerate their importance and achievements far beyond credibility," wrote Klaus Hinrichsen. "Listening to him one would think that the accumulation of talent in Hutchinson Camp had only twice been equalled in history: in antiquity in Athens under Pericles, and in Renaissance Florence under the Medici. Be that as it may, a surprised Captain Daniel promptly saw the need for materials for 'his' artists, and even more importantly, the need for studio space. In return Oppenheimer promised an art exhibition the like of which had not been seen in any other internment camp on the island."

The exhibition opened on September 14, 1940, and its impact on the artists was such that one, Fred Uhlman, described it as "the best day since my internment." After spending nearly two months foraging for materials wherever they could around the square, these men were given an opportunity to do something that was an integral part of their lives. Kurt Schwitters walked the room where his latest oil paintings now hung alongside woodcuts by Hellmuth Weissenborn, wood figures by Ernst Müller-Blensdorf, portraits by Gerhard Ehrlich, and drawings by Fritz Salomonski, Eric (Ernst) Stern, and Uhlman.

"To summarize the impression after visiting the Camp's Art Exhibition: It is astounding and encouraging to see how the artists under the given conditions did not loose [sic] heart," wrote a correspondent called A. Z. in The Camp on September 29. "This first Art Exhibition showed what extraordinary high standard, both in quality and quantity, is concentrated in this camp. . . . This colorful display spoke more eloquently than any words [about] how many artists were obliged to leave a country where the spirit of art is employed as the mere tool of propaganda."

That last point was emphasized, in particular, by the contribution of Paul Hamann to the exhibition, a World War I veteran of the German army, and a sculptor whose life masks of the likes of Man Ray were so famous that, ironically, he had been commissioned in 1930 to make one of Winston Churchill's wife, Clementine. Hamann's escape from the Nazis took him to Paris first and then London. Unable to produce anything in time for the opening show at Hutchinson, he brought along photographs of some of his previous work which had been on prominent public display in Germany before the rise of Hitler.

The exhibition was such an unqualified success that Commander Daniel immediately announced a second show for later in the year, even as many of the artists featured were also busy trying to negotiate their release. To this end, fifteen of them had already written an open letter to Kenneth Clark, director of the National Gallery, imploring him to vouch for them, their work, and their bona fides. They were irked that the government White Paper gave eighteen different categories of internees eligible for release but made no mention of artists. Since that publication advised scientists or researchers seeking release to canvas the president of the Royal Society or the president of the British Academy, they identified Clark as a man who might take up the cudgel on their behalf.

"It is hardly necessary to point out to you that we refugee artists have come to this country," they wrote on August 8, 1940, "because the freedom of our artistic conscience and creative intelligence was threatened, nay, annihilated by the tyranny of the Nazi government in Germany as well as in the countries invaded by the Germans, such as Austria, Norway, the Netherlands, etc., to which some of us had fled from Nazi oppression.

"There are men amongst us whose works, adorning the public places and building for which they had been commissioned and executed, were smashed, blown up, and defaced by the Nazi oppressors, and who have thus been more deeply wounded and hurt than if they had been subjected to bodily ill-treatment. They have come to this country in order to breathe the air of freedom without which art cannot thrive. . . . Could you not, and would you not, Sir, exert your influence with the Advisory Committee set up by the Home Office, so as to obtain the inclusion of artists among the categories of internees eligible for release?"

The letter was signed by Ernst M. Blensdorf, Kurt Schwitters, Ernst Schwitters, Siegfried Charoux, Paul Hamann, Fritz Kraemer, Hermann Roessler, Carl Felkel, Fred Uhlman, Erich Kahn, Fred Solomonski, Eric (Ernst) Stern, Georg Ehrlich, Hellmuth Weissenborn, and Hermann Fechenbach.

Clark's reply took three weeks and was the measured response of a man who appreciated the injustice yet realized the limits of his own power.

"Gentlemen, I have delayed answering your letter as I had hoped it would be possible for me to give you some good news, but it is still very difficult to find out what section of the Home Office is responsible for adding artists to the categories of internees who may be liberated," he wrote. "I have, however, written to Mr. Justice Asquith, Chairman of the Advisory Committee, and hope that I shall be able to appear before this Committee and persuade them to add artists to the eighteen categories. . . . I will gladly do all I can to help you."

Beseeching a man of influence to do what he could was a smart move. Of course, among the signatories to the letter sent to Clark was Fred Uhlman, an individual with an even more direct line to somebody far more politically powerful than the erstwhile director of the National Gallery. Uhlman was married to Diana Croft, whose father, Brigadier-General Sir Henry Page Croft, had, earlier that year, been appointed under-secretary of state for war by Winston Churchill. That his father-in-law had the ear of the prime minister might have counted for something, except for the fact that Croft hated Germans and Jews with a passion. Uhlman was both.

The story of how Fred Uhlman ended up in England has a more romantic tinge to it than the narratives involving his fellow internees. Born into a Jewish family of merchants in Stuttgart in 1901, though reared in a secular house, he studied law at Freiburg, Munich, and Tübingen before returning to his hometown to practice in 1927. He became active in the Social Democratic Party, traveling to towns like Ulm and Reutlingen with security guards protecting him during the 1933 elections. Indeed, his office on Archivstrasse was election headquarters, and almost everybody that slept there the night before voting was armed, an indication of how much they feared for the results, and their lives. Within days of the Nazi victory, a judge of his acquaintance told a friend to warn him, "If you see Uhlmannle [little Uhlman], tell him that Paris is very beautiful now. Tell him: *now!*"

Uhlman took the advice, moving to the French capital where his cousin, Paul Elsas, was carving out a reputation as a painter. Uhlman had dabbled in painting merely as a hobby, but now, deprived of the ability to use his legal qualifications, and encouraged by Elsas and Paul Westheim, an émigré German art critic, he threw himself into the production of paintings. That he was also hanging around the fabled Café du Dome in Montparnasse—the epicenter of artistic and literary life in

Paris, boasting clientele and alumni like Pablo Picasso, Man Ray, Henri Cartier-Bresson, and Amedeo Modigliani—probably helped too.

In a city full of struggling artists (forty thousand, by his own estimate), Uhlman, showcasing a primitive, self-taught style, was always going to find it hard to make money. He supplemented his income with some minor art dealing and a stint selling tropical fish. At his first one-man show early in 1936, he didn't sell a single piece, and financial reality made his stay in Paris no longer tenable. Oskar Zugel, a painter he knew from Stuttgart, invited him to the Spanish fishing village of Tossa de Mar, where, he was assured, the living was cheap.

He arrived on April Fool's Day, 1936, three months before the outbreak of the Spanish Civil War. While there, he met and fell in love with Diana Croft. She had arrived in Spain at the wheel of a Lagonda motorcar, accompanied by her friend Betty Sackville-West, a pair of intrepid travelers from well-established English families traversing Europe in search of adventure and excitement. She found that and more in a country on the brink when her future husband asked her to dance in a bar.

After a brief flirtation with going to Barcelona to join the International Brigade, Uhlman fled back to France, where Croft came to meet him in Paris. From there, they went to England. He spoke no English and, as he later admitted, "If it had been China, I could not have known less about the country." The relationship caused an immediate stir in high society, one of her cousins reporting back that Diana had been seen with "a little Jew in Kew Gardens." The couple got engaged within weeks, at which point Uhlman was summoned to an interview with his future father-in-law, Brigadier-General Sir Henry Paul Croft.

A Member of Parliament since 1910, synonymous with the far-right wing of the Conservative Party, Croft espoused such an extreme brand of nationalism and imperialism that he briefly broke away from the Tories to lead the National Party. Its platform included "the exclusion of all undesirable aliens and expulsion of all German and Bolshevik influence" from Britain. Near the end of World War I, he led a demonstration to 10 Downing Street calling for the internment of all enemy aliens, and was on record as believing the Russian Revolution was a German-Jewish conspiracy.

He didn't like Germans or Jews, and here before him was a German Jew who also happened to be near enough destitute. Before the interrogation (conducted by an interpreter) began, Uhlman was treated to a recital of the Croft history, this being a family that boasted nearly five centuries of parliamentary service and traced its illustrious lineage back to the Domesday Book and William the Conqueror in 1087. If the intention was to show him the pedigree of people he was dealing with, the history lesson meant very little to Uhlman, who had reached his mid-thirties without ever knowing anything about the Domesday Book. Even with a language barrier, he quickly realized the lie of the land.

"To him, I was a foreigner who had hurt him in his pride and spoilt his hopes of his daughter marrying some distinguished Englishman. I was déclassé, uprooted, and, in almost every respect the last kind of person he cared to know," wrote Uhlman. "I think that I must have been everything he loathed most: He hated Germans and Socialists and Jews, and probably disliked artists too."

Ever the rebel and a committed socialist herself, Diana was not put off by her father's disapproval. Au contraire, she may well have been emboldened by it. The two were married on November 4 in a registry office in London, long before the six-month waiting period Sir Henry had requested. Although the English press did not hear of the ceremony, a Stuttgart newspaper ran a conspiracy theory–esque story about Uhlman, "the well-known Marxist and Jew" now becoming part of the British establishment.

In reality, Uhlman had taken legal steps to divest himself of any claim to his wife's fortune, and the couple—she was a gifted linguist—threw themselves into various causes, working on behalf of Republicans in Spain during the Civil War and getting involved in the Artists' Refugee Committee, a group working to assist German artists trying to escape the growing reach of the Nazis around Europe. They were also both key figures in the Free German League of Culture, a body aiming to unite exiled refugees so they could work together to counter Nazi propaganda and influence.

In July 1939, the league's first exhibition was held at the Wertheim Gallery where, in a positive review of the work of a host of refugee artists, Jan Gordon in *The Observer* praised Uhlman's paintings for "speaking simplicities." When war broke out, the executive committee of the league wrote to the Home Office, offering their services "in the defense of Freedom, Culture and Democracy," and Uhlman signed up to join the Air Raid Precautions (ARP) organization as a warden in December 1939, patrolling streets during blackouts, a role that freed him up to paint during the day.

As Uhlman did his bit for the war effort, his father-in-law was asking questions in Parliament about exactly how many Jewish refugees were entering Britain and its dominions. By the end of June 1940, Diana was heavily pregnant, and the couple was staying with her aunt in Ware when a pair of policemen knocked at the door and took Fred away to be interned. After a couple of weeks at the Bertram Mills' Circus winter headquarters camp in Ascot, he arrived on the Isle of Man and walked up the hill toward Hutchinson Camp, a couple of days after his father-in-law had once more been banging the drum for internment in the House of Commons.

On the surface, being related to a man serving in Churchill's War Cabinet gave Uhlman some hope that his stay on the island might still be brief. Having given birth to their first child, Caroline, on July 3, Diana immediately contacted her father and asked him to intercede on Fred's behalf. Croft wrote to the Home Office, reminding them that Uhlman was anti-Hitler and hardly a threat, but also making it clear that if his internment was part of the general "Collar the lot!" sweep, he had no problem with the decision.

"There is no record, however, that would testify to any attempt by Croft to speed up Uhlman's release despite the fact that his cabinet post would have enabled him to mobilize forces to have his son-in-law released as quickly as possible," wrote Anna Muller-Harlin. "A desperate Uhlman himself then approached Croft in a letter. . . . However, his humble call for help did not soften Croft's standpoint."

Uhlman kept a diary of his internment, a document that allows us a window into the quotidian routine of the men, including such matters as grumbling about sharing living space. Uhlman was greatly peeved when Rolf Runkel, an intelligence officer in the German Communist Party, moved into his room. "The blond beast," as Uhlman called him, was actually a Soviet spy who had been recruited by the NKVD and was by then on a Gestapo wanted list. He did, however, turn out to be uncommonly neat, compared to Uhlman's previous roommate, Carl Ludwig Franck.

While Uhlman threw himself into his art, managing a couple of hundred drawings, he also struggled with depression and not knowing just how long he was to remain incarcerated. Witness a sample of diary entries written over the course of six weeks:

September 7: Again this terrible, ghastly, sickening depression. Nothing will help. No courage, nor logic. The black cloud will not disperse. I hate seeing people. Rumors about bad air-raids over London, which can only mean I will not be released for weeks and weeks.

October 12: Wellesz, Ehrlich, Pariser, released. I am glad for them, but what about me? Why can I, who deserved it more than they who never did anything against the Nazis, not be released? . . . Can hardly sleep and don't want to eat. Hate the whole place more than ever.

October 22: Beautiful October day. Try to fight depression by telling myself that millions suffer more, that I am damned lucky to be alive, that I am a bloody coward, a spoiled man who has—compared to others—a good life. Nothing helps. Reason is powerless. If only I had a date—You'll be free in six months, six years—I could settle. But the uncertainty is so hard to bear.

The only thing that made the place bearable was the art and the artists. He was smitten by Schwitters, as much for his larger-than-life personality that livened up every day as for his technical ability. The pair became fast friends, and Uhlman never tired of hearing him spin the same outlandish yarns over and over again. Aside from Schwitters, he formed other strong relationships, too, recalling several lengthy conversations with, among others, Georg Ehrlich, the renowned Austrian sculptor who was also a World War I veteran; Professor Paul Jacobsthal;

and Professor William Cohn. He is also credited with coming up with the idea of creating a space for the artists and other kindred spirits in the camp to gather.

"I rather suspect it was Fred Uhlman forever hankering after the Café Dome in Paris who found a house with a superb Viennese pastry cook, who was willing to let out the house's laundry room for a couple of hours in the afternoons," wrote Hinrichsen. "There is a drawing by Uhlman in this exhibition, showing the laundry room with the inmates' long-johns hanging from the ceiling, and presumably dripping into the coffee, and the long table around which the artists were sitting. There also exists a thinly disguised account of these proceedings in Richard Friedenthal's book *Die Welt in der Nussschale*, which appeared in Germany in the fifties. I can't remember how one qualified for membership, nor why I was accepted from the beginning. Art historians are viewed with suspicion by artists—you know the quip 'Those who can, do, those who can't, criticize!' . . . Those afternoons in the Artists' Café were dominated by two brilliant raconteurs: Fred Uhlman, with his stories about running a tropical fish business in Paris, and Kurt Schwitters with his stammerer poems."

Hinrichsen gathered the signatures of all the men present at the Artists' Café one November afternoon and there were thirty-four names on the list. It says much for the ecumenical approach of those involved that the attendees that day included writers, poets, graphologists, musicians, and architects. Rules of membership appear to have been quite lax, although there was one strict diktat: Nobody was ever allowed to use the word "release." Since that topic dominated nearly every waking minute for the internees, it was hoped that in the café they could forget that preoccupation and instead talk about loftier matters.

There were two notable absentees from the community that clustered together in the laundry room they had convinced themselves was a Parisian café. The first was Ludwig Meidner, a famous expressionist who, like Schwitters, had had his work condemned by the Nazis and featured in the "Degenerate Art" exhibitions. Conscripted into the German military during the first war, Meidner had, ironically, been put to work then as an interpreter and a censor at a prisoner-of-war camp. At Hutchinson, he kept himself so anonymous that Hinrichsen, the unofficial camp chronicler, didn't even known Meidner was a fellow internee until after the war.

The reason may have been that Meidner arrived in the camp in a later wave, transferring from Huyton in November of 1940. It could also have been put down to the fact that he was, at this stage of his life, deeply religious, and spent most of his time in one of the Orthodox Jewish houses in the square. On something of a spiritual odyssey, he had, at various times, been an atheist, a socialist revolutionary, a Marxist, and a devotee of Christian mysticism, before returning to the faith into which he had been born in Silesia back in 1884.

"I am connected with the Orthodox group here, and yet am alone here where there is less intelligence and cheer [than in the camp at Huyton]," wrote Meidner in a letter to friends during his stay.

Uhlman did have some contact with Meidner while sitting for a portrait sketch. During one of those encounters, Meidner confessed he had grown so content with his new surroundings that he "implored me to do everything in my power to stop him [from being] released." Little wonder. Over the course of a fecund year and a half behind barbed wire at various locations, he produced thirteen sketchbooks filled with work.

Hermann Fechenbach never attended the café either, and, according to Hinrichsen, this may have been due to a combination of his prickly temperament, his resentment that the more established artists were fussed over, and the fact that he struggled with the concept of internment. There was also the small matter of a feud between the pair. Nobody remembers what the bad blood was about, but it was Fechenbach who offered to make peace, eventually asking his nemesis to sit for a portrait. Hinrichsen sat for three mornings in a row and was not thrilled with the end result.

"It was a picture of a whole house, and I was looking out of one of the windows," said Hinrichsen. "And the size of my portrait, was, if anything, half an inch. I think he wanted to show what he thought of me, but . . . eventually we got friendly."

Fechenbach was forty-three years old when he arrived at Hutchinson. A native of Bad Mergentheim, he lost his left leg fighting for Germany in World War I; he also lost a flourishing career as a painter and graphic artist in Stuttgart to the rise of the Nazis. For a time in the mid-1930s, he devoted himself to helping fellow Jews in that city learn the skills they would need to flourish once they got out of the country. He and his wife, Greta Batze, emigrated to Palestine in 1938, but, unhappy with the instability of the political situation there, they moved to England a year later.

Fechenbach immediately began working as a painter and engraver in London, using the money to finance his parents' passage to join his brothers, freshly arrived in Argentina. His twin sister Rosa did not escape in time and was killed in a concentration camp. That background may explain why his work, perhaps more than any other, was the most nakedly political and the most obviously a product of the peculiar circumstances. Indeed, before he even got to the Isle of Man, he'd organized a hunger strike to protest the conditions at the infamous Warth Mills transit camp, and produced eerie linocuts to showcase the horrors that the men living there were forced to endure.

He continued to use linocuts when he got to Hutchinson, where somebody had pressed an old laundry mangle into service once they discovered it could apply enough pressure to make prints. Strips of lino were sliced from kitchen and bathroom floors using cutlery, and the technology allowed men like Fechenbach to make multiple copies of their best pieces. One of his most memorable images—a group of men huddled in front of barbed wire, watching somebody on the other side depart—is known as *Waiting*, or, alternatively, *Released*, each title allowing the piece to be viewed differently.

Fechenbach did show his work in both of the camp exhibitions, and the second was so anticipated that on November 19, 1940, it merited a front-page preview in *The Camp*.

"This exhibition is more than a mere collection of drawings, paintings, sculptures, and so forth. It is a sign, a signal, and a challenge to everybody here," wrote Michael Corvin. "Go on with your work as well you can; and if you cannot do anything in your old line, try a new one. . . . It will help you not only to keep your chin up, but to strengthen your mind and your resolution, to overcome everything by creating in the way given to you."

Apart from impacting on the men's morale and confirming Daniel's notions of superiority, the exhibitions also served another purpose. In December of 1940 when the artists of the camp wrote to the Artists' Refugee Committee in London, campaigning for the release of Erich Kahn, another who suffered badly from depression, they cited his contributions to both shows.

"We therefore wish to stress that Kahn has done some excellent work during internment, utilizing various techniques such as pencil drawing, red chalk drawing, monotypes, etchings, and oil paintings. In the two exhibitions arranged in this Camp, works exhibited by him were of outstanding quality and showed an impressive artistic talent. . . . Having arrived in this country only shortly before the outbreak of war, unable to bring with him any criticisms from papers, etc. . . . he has only saved few works from Germany, and was, therefore, never able to exhibit in this country."

The artists didn't live in isolation. Others were inspired by their example to try their own hand at creating. H. G. Gussefeld, a businessman with no previous experience at creating art—or, indeed, making anything—watched Fechenbach at work and then carved an exquisite wooden crocodile from a tent peg he had brought with him from Prees Heath Camp.

The artists' influence was even more pronounced in the case of Peter Fleischmann, the youngest member of their circle. Like Hans Furth among the older musicians, he was regarded as something of a protégé by men like Schwitters, Hamann, and Ehrlich, in particular, and he soaked up knowledge from all of these talented and experienced practitioners. Several photographs exist of Fleischmann hard at work. One shows him sculpting a wooden figure as Hamann stands over his shoulder, poised to instruct, both men puffing on pipes, wisps of clouds rising in the studio.

Fleischmann had spent most of his life in a Berlin orphanage following the death of his parents in a car crash that took the lives of several prominent socialist journalists and had the whiff of something sinister about it. In his mid-teens, he turned up on the Gestapo's radar and was briefly on the run before snagging a seat on one of the earliest kindertransports to Britain. His arrival at Harwich was captured by a

Pathé newsreel camera, extant footage showing a diffident teen arriving in a place where his historic failure to pay attention in English class was suddenly going to prove costly.

On government orders, an uncle of his in Manchester took him in, but did so under duress. That much was made clear in the bathroom, where the German boy was allotted old newspaper rather than the toilet tissue reserved for the family. Eventually, he got lodgings of his own and a job in a photographic company, where he befriended another teen, Donald Midgley. Midgley brought the refugee boy home to his family on the weekends to be fed and looked after. When casting around for a more English surname a decade later, Fleischmann took theirs as a gesture of appreciation for their kindness, and it was as Peter Midgley that he ultimately gained fame and recognition.

After war was declared in September 1939, the two lads went to sign up together. Donald Midgley was taken by the Royal Air Force, but Fleischmann was rejected outright. Soon, he was before a tribunal and eventually interned. Following stops at Warth Mills and Prees Heath, he arrived at Hutchinson at the end of the summer of 1940, by which time the artistic community there was already thriving. For somebody who had left Berlin in a hurry, yet still carefully carrying his teenage artwork under his arm, here was a unique opportunity to breathe the same air as giants. In most cases, extremely accommodating, big, friendly giants.

"I remember the talks Fred Uhlman gave me, personally, about the world outside England, and the arts," said Fleischmann. "Kurt Schwitters gave life drawing classes, and he taught me how to make my own paints from ground-down bricks, showed me that anything with colour could be used. It was my first introduction to sculpture, under Georg Ehrlich, who showed me how to cast, and Paul Hamann. Technically, everything I got from art college after the war was just a recap. I was given a lot of information in that short time."

The lessons included ingenuity. Fleischmann dug his own clay to sculpt with, repurposed brown paper from parcels as canvases, and tore the hard covers off of old books to paint on. That was the spirit of the artistic community in Hutchinson. When a fresh batch of firewood arrived, these men sifted through it in search of promising pieces that might be hewed into something memorable. Decades later, Fleischmann recalled Ernst Müller-Blensdorf working with chairs and piano legs, and even tearing a door off in his house so he could have something to carve.

Their generosity of spirit to the neophyte in their midst set Fleischmann up for a life in art, and may explain why he was not in a hurry to leave. Indeed, it was the commander who eventually applied for his release without him even knowing about it. Even after he had departed, Fleischmann's attitude toward life in the camp and its effect on him was, inevitably, a lot more positive than most others.

"One couldn't just wish for any more," he said. "I had nobody outside pining or waiting for me or queuing up for me. What an introduction to people, artists, painting, culture, concerts—stuff I'd have to pay a fortune for at any other time. I was made. I was made. It was the beginning of my life. The making of my life."

CHAPTER THIRTEEN

Catch and Release

Well, I shall never forget this period of my life. It sometimes occurs that periods of one's life happen to be forgotten, as if they were fallen into a deep black well—and I think my future life will be directed by it. . . . Once I am released I shall be free, free again, and really free when I save and keep that feeling of freedom, of all these inner values gained in internment, into reality, into daily routine work of our outside world. That perhaps is my adventure of internment, the lesson it taught me. Therefore, it is my internment, it belongs to me, to the development of my personality. I wouldn't miss it.
—ULLI HIRSCH, NOVEMBER 1940

ON SEPTEMBER 4, 1940, A CROWD OF SEVERAL HUNDRED INTERNEES gathered near the barbed wire to watch a wedding ceremony take place in the orderly room that lay on the other side. Ernst L. Bodenheimer, a native of Frankfurt, Germany, had received a special dispensation from the commander to marry a compatriot, Miss Clementine Eisemann (then of Stoke Newington), because their entry visas for Cuba required them to be a couple. Bodenheimer had a brother who emigrated to the United States in the 1920s, and that was where he ultimately hoped to land.

Earlier that morning, Bodenheimer had been escorted out of the camp and down the hill into Douglas where his wife to be, granted special permission to come to the island, was waiting at the registry office on

Athol Street. Bodenheimer was accompanied by a government official, Mr. Latham, an officer of the camp, and a soldier. When they emerged onto the street after the civil ceremony, one newspaper reported that the couple looked "very happy and were wearing flowers."

Their return to Hutchinson Square prompted some excitement, the men obviously keen for any distraction most days. Internees gathered to observe from afar the religious wedding service to be held at the camp's administrative building, just the other side of the fencing. Dr. Robert Marshall, the camp physician, had ensured there would be flowers in the orderly room. "All the religious rites were observed," wrote the *Ramsey Courier*, "and at the end of the ceremony the bridegroom crushed a glass to bits."

When the couple emerged, the men on the other side of the barbed wire cheered, many shouting *Mazel tov!* at the newlyweds. An unusual wedding day by any standards, it ended differently, too. Bodenheimer returned to his house on Hutchinson Square, and an hour after being married, the new Mrs. Bodenheimer was taken to the island's airport, from where she flew back to the mainland alone. It would be at least two weeks before her husband's release could be authorized. The couple eventually made it to New York, and their marriage lasted sixty years, until Ernst's death in 2000.

Marriage was Bodenheimer's way out. For everybody else, release and how to secure it was on their mind from the moment they walked in the gate to the morning they left. Indeed, according to one legend, Kurt Schwitters's son Ernst applied for release on the grounds that lack of sex was starting to make his teeth loosen.

Some did not have to go to such ludicrous lengths to have their papers stamped.

Witness the tale of Walter Neurath, who fit the same profile as many internees. He had a flourishing professional career in Vienna before the Anschluss, after which his life and work were upended by the Nazis. A member of a left-wing intellectual commune called *Neustift* (New Foundations) in the early 1920s, he spent much of the 1930s publishing anti-Nazi literature, the kind of work that had the Gestapo quickly on his trail. He fled to England in 1938 with his second wife, Marianne, their entry sponsored by Frances Margesson, wife of the Conservative MP for Rugby and chief whip in the British government.

In London, Neurath found work as a production manager at Adprint and was centrally involved in the multivolume collection, *Britain in Pictures*. His contribution to that gargantuan and acclaimed project is why he spent just two weeks on the Isle of Man. Somebody in a position of influence was informed that his input was essential to a series of books then regarded as useful propaganda tools. As Neurath readied himself to leave, Wilhelm Feuchtwang, a fellow Viennese who had befriended him during their short time together at Hutchinson, asked him for help.

Feuchtwang's wife Eva and infant son Stephan remained in London when he was arrested, and were in a precarious financial position. He beseeched Neurath to go check on their well-being. After going to see them, Neurath secured Eva a job at Adprint. The pair became colleagues and good friends. Eventually, after she divorced Wilhelm, the two married and became renowned as the power couple behind Thames and Hudson, a publishing house synonymous with high-end art books over the rest of the twentieth century.

If securing release was a preoccupation for most of the men, most of the time, they also contemplated various apocalyptic scenarios in terms of the course of the war raging in Europe. Chief among the most dreaded outcomes was the Nazis invading the British mainland, or the island of Ireland. Either of those eventualities would surely bring the conflict to Douglas, too.

"We were all afraid of what would happen to our wives and children if the country was invaded," said Fritz Hallgarten. "And if the Nazis landed in Ireland or the Isle of Man, what would happen to us? So, we formed a little group, eight or ten people, and decided we'd steal a boat somewhere in the island and we'd go to England or to America. We'd drift somewhere, some way, and not be caught by the Nazis like rats in the cage. We at least wanted to fight. We would have cut the barbed wire, got out of the camp, and did something. We might have died on the Isle of Man, but we'd die fighting."

Ronald Stent encountered similar spirit, noting that "[o]thers advocated a last desperate stand, such as the Spartans at Thermopylae."

Heinrich Fraenkel recalled another debate in which internees discussed a prospective Nazi invasion of the island, something that obviously seemed a very real possibility in the minds of the men. Fraenkel openly admitted that he'd secreted away a sharp razor blade so that he could end his own life in that circumstance. This revelation offended another German resident with personal experience of interrogation by the Gestapo.

"Razor blade be damned," said the man from Silesia. "If those swine should catch me again I wouldn't do their blasted job for them. I would bloody well make 'em spend one of their precious bullets on me—and, by God, I should use that last minute to tell 'em what I think of them. Maybe it would give one of those bastards something to think about, after all!"

The men were often confused and resentful about the situation of their internment and the ongoing puzzle of how to quickly effect their release. Despite the various editions of the government White Paper attempting to clarify the process, residents were perplexed by the manner in which some were released earlier than others. For instance, the first men got their tickets out stamped under Paragraph 19, which recognized prominent anti-Hitler activists, only in early November.

"The order in which they came out and sometimes the reasons why were utterly unapparent," wrote Paul Jacobsthal. "One day a sick man and a rabbi, the next an old man and one in whom a bishop took an interest (another rabbi), then an agricultural worker, a boy employed by the Royal Automobile Club, and a destitute who was sorry to leave and did not know on what he was going to live. Of our set, only Professor Weigert, the chemophysicist, was early-released, either because his work was considered to be of national importance or because the Home Office had satisfied itself that a man who is stone deaf would hardly be able to communicate with parachutists."

Jacobsthal struggled, in particular, with how German academics had been swept up in Oxford yet German dentists in the town remained at large. Like Hallgarten, he was occasionally pressed into service as a scribe by less well-educated colleagues who figured the fastest way off the island was to send letters to any prominent person they believed might sway their case at the Home Office.

Others provided a flourish of their own.

Emil Mauer, a socialist and former mayor of Vienna, wrote to Herbert Morrison, whom he'd met long before the war through their mutual work with Socialist International, asking for help. To illustrate the folly of his situation and to make his case for release from Hutchinson, he signed the letter, "Mauer, internee of [Kurt] Schusnigg's [fascist chancellor in 1930s Austria], then of Hitler's, and now of [Clement] Attlee's concentration camps," pointedly blaming his plight on Morrison's Labor Party colleague, who was Lord Privy Seal in Churchill's War Cabinet.

The inevitable obsession with the hows and whys of release prompted inside jokes.

"This was the time when Gandhi, the Mahatma, was very much in the news; he too had been interned during the war," wrote Ronald Stent. "The favorite catchphrase at Hutchinson became 'Ma-hat-ma released,' an Austrian variant of the proper German, '*Man hat mich* released,' often an expression of wishful thinking."

Once the regular releases started to come, something of a ritual attended the departure of each man from his particular house. Cooks hoarded flour to make cakes for the inevitable farewell party the night before. Then, on the morning the person was to leave the camp forever, his gaggle of friends accompanied him all the way to the barbed wire. While some felt pangs of envy as they saw others' numbers being called before theirs (Fred Uhlman admitted as much in his diary), most seemed to have found some solace in the fact that good men were getting to return to society.

"He talked to each of us and spoke with words of hope and strength," wrote Michael Corvin, of the departure of one of his housemates who was emigrating to Palestine. "He took our hands and embraced us and kissed us farewell. He stammered, words failing almost with emotion as he was blessing his friends. Little Joseph, our parting friend, felt it; he was certain that this was the irreversible parting. A farewell for life, and forever. He formed his words with a heavy voice and nodded to stress them as tears appeared in his eyes. And when the gate opened he pushed forward and rushed out. Now it became too difficult. It had to happen quickly so that it was done. In the dawn the boat with smoking funnels was lying at the pier. Soft rain was falling and we walked back to the house which had become emptier."

Corvin himself later emigrated to California.

Some people departed the camp and left their memory of the time and place behind. Others, however, carried the knowledge that they had been wronged, their reputations impugned by the very act of their internment. In 1946, Captain Harry Cemach of the Royal Army Ordnance Corps was aboard the SS *Carthage* returning to Britain to be demobilized. About to return to life as a chartered accountant and a future in which he'd write several textbooks about the conduct of the modern business office, and another about the Indonesian language, he sat down in the drawing room of the ship one day to write a letter to the *Isle of Man Times*.

Here was a sequel to his first missive in October 1940, a reminder that everything he wrote the first time about the injustice of that newspaper labeling internees as "Huns" (see chapter 6) had been borne out by subsequent events during the course of the conflict.

"On my epaulettes, there are the three 'pips' of a captain in His Majesty's Army; on my jacket the colored ribbon commemorating the defense of Britain and the Burma Campaign," wrote Cemach. "I write this letter because I know that by publishing it—and this time I know you will publish it, whilst back in 1940, I didn't really expect you to print my letter—you will be squaring off a debt which you still owe me, and I believe you will be glad to do so. If I ask you to print my story it is not because mine is the most heroic of the stories that could be written."

He went on to recount the tales of so many former "enemy aliens" who had suffered internment in the early years of the war before, upon release, serving with distinction in the cause of defeating Hitler and his allies. While Cemach carved out a military career of solid service, he was aware that his contribution paled next to others.

"And, sir, my story means little compared with that of my dear friend Freddy Fleischer who shared internment with me in Douglas, back in

1940. Freddy joined the Pioneer Corps when I did, and later—when given an opportunity to do so—volunteered for transfer to the Commandos. He trained with them, then took part in the invasion of France, and was killed not long after D-Day. He lies buried there, with his comrades, a British soldier."

Cemach reminded the editor of the *Times* about the "humiliation" he and his peers had endured when they were locked up, their psychological conditions worsened by the arrival in camp of the island's most prominent newspaper, replete with articles describing these men, these refugees from Hitler, as "Huns." He went on to point out that during his stay behind barbed wire, he never lost sight of the fact that his own real enemy was not "in the Home Office in Whitehall or in the editorial office of your paper in Douglas, but in Berlin."

"Wasn't it time, sir," he asked, "that in the true spirit of British fair play, you faced up to facts and honestly unashamed, nay—proudly— stood up and said: 'We were wrong in those days, you have kept faith and we acknowledge it.'"

The *Isle of Man Times* did just that by printing the letter.

What is astonishing is how so many of the internees recovered from the ordeal, resumed their lives interrupted, and then went on to leave indelible marks in so many different fields. Cemach was not well-known, yet his literary output is part of a recurring theme among his one-time neighbors. Dozens of the men wrote books of one sort or another, from novels to memoirs to academic tomes to business organization manuals. Half a dozen of the artists had books written about them (scores, indeed, about Schwitters alone), while perhaps the most graphic illustration of the impact of Rawicz and Landauer is that in March 1961 they were the subjects of BBC Television's *This Is Your Life*, a singular accolade accorded only to those who have made a unique contribution to British society and popular culture.

Hans Brick returned to the circus world from which he came, serving as menagerie manager for Chipperfield's Circus in Britain for much of the 1950s, while also doing occasional turns as a highly regarded clown act. He remained a figure of such renown that when a leopard in his retinue allowed him into her cage to pet her newly born cubs, the story flashed across the international newswires. He wrote two books about his relationships with animals. After the 1962 publication of *The Nature of the Beast*, one American reviewer considered Brick's feats with his lion Habibi, his prowess with so many different creatures, and wondered if he was "one of the world's exceptional characters."

Others achieved recognition in a different way. Upon release, Adolf Mirecki did not use the artistic talents evinced in his satiric contributions to *The Camp* as DOL. Having spent time in Hong Kong and South Africa during the war, he returned to England, married Mary Colbourn, and had three children. He also established Shuresta, an innovative company building prams, baby carriages, child car seats, and bicycle stands at a factory in Exhall, just outside Coventry. Not long after being deemed an enemy alien, he was employing four hundred people in the Midlands.

Hans Furth, the prodigy in Hutchinson's musical fraternity, had a stint as a piano teacher at a Quaker school in York and worked as a farmhand before entering St. Hugh's, a Carthusian monastery at Parkminster, in Sussex. ("I met some Carthusians on the Isle of Man, that's why!") He lived as an ascetic for seven years before moving to Canada, his emigration made possible by the fact he was now a British subject. In Montreal, he worked in a mental hospital, supplemented his income by giving piano recitals and lessons, and studied for a master's in clinical psychology and then a PhD in experimental psychology at Portland State University in Oregon.

Like so many, Furth seemed determined to wring the most out of his post-Hutchinson life. He taught at Catholic University in Washington, DC, from 1960 to 1990, writing ten books, including the acclaimed *Thinking Without Language: Psychological Implications of Deafness*. A frequent collaborator with Jean Piaget, whom he met while on sabbatical in Geneva in the mid-1960s, he is widely credited with popularizing the Swiss psychologist's theories about child development with his best-selling *Piaget and Knowledge: Theoretical Foundations*.

Furth died from a heart attack suffered while hiking in Shenandoah National Park at the age of seventy-nine. He was survived by seven children, and had just completed a manuscript called *Society Faces Extinction: The Psychology of Auschwitz and Hiroshima*.

If the Pioneer Corps was Ronald Stent's ticket out of the camp and off the island, he made the most of every opportunity thereafter, picking up an officer's commission and serving on the staff of GHG India in New Delhi. While sipping gin and tonic on the terrace of the Gymkhana club there one afternoon in 1944, having just played tennis with the brigadier's wife, he had an epiphany. "I thought back to how just four years before I had been gazing wistfully at the barbed-wire strands of Hutchinson Camp and at the deep blue sea beyond," wrote Stent. "Life certainly had changed since then. Those five months had been a strange experience, harsh, testing, stimulating, not a bad preparation for what came afterwards. The memory of the unpleasant aspects and experiences had already faded. . . . It had, after all, not been a wasted period, not a bad time."

That was the final paragraph of *A Bespattered Page? The Internment of His Majesty's "Most Loyal Enemy Aliens,"* Stent's definitive account of what he and his peers at Hutchinson and other camps had been through during World War II. Pieced together from interviews with eyewitnesses, it was published in 1980, by which time he had, after retiring from a successful international business career, become a historian. He was still teaching part-time at age ninety, and by then, his daughter Monica wrote, "was a Pukka English gentleman."

Stent's friendship with Fritz Hallgarten, which preceded their time in camp, endured for the rest of their lives. The welfare officer returned to his wife in Kings Langley in time for Christmas 1940, immediately applied for the Home Guard, and then made a unique contribution to the war effort. A friend from the intelligence services came looking for any German clothes or paraphernalia that could be given to spies trying to pass themselves off in foreign territory. He cleared out the loft, putting together a package that included German pencils, socks, shirts, ties, and old train tickets. He was confident that anybody dropped behind enemy lines in this garb would come across very Hallgarten.

Over the ensuing decades, he became one of the most influential figures in the British wine industry through the House of Hallgarten. In a profile in 1971, John Arlott described him as "the best nose in the wine business." His competitors were much less complimentary when he

published *Wine Scandal* in 1986, a scathing exposé of some of the fraud-
ulent practices that went into producing the most popular vintages.

After a brief stint as chair of the Royal Irish Academy in Dublin, Dr.
Gerhard Bersu returned to Frankfurt to his old position at the German
Archaeological Institute, where he contributed hugely to its ongoing
reorganization and rebuilding. Shortly before his retirement in 1956, one
of his last acts was supervising the reopening of the institution, a fitting
monument to the defiance and courage he had displayed when the Nazis
came calling.

Aside from *The World in a Nutshell*, his fictional account of life in
the camp, Richard Friedenthal wrote heavyweight tomes about Mar-
tin Luther, Leonardo da Vinci, and Handel, and the *New York Times*
described his work on Goethe as "the best biography of Goethe in
English." He remained in England after the war and worked for the
BBC (the definition of an establishment job), and also served as honorary
chairman of the PEN Center for German-Speaking Authors Abroad.

Hellmuth Weissenborn had provided fifteen wood engravings to
illustrate Friedenthal's *Goethe Chronicle* in 1949, a collaboration that was
the fruit of another friendship formed in internment. By that point in his
own career, Weissenborn, his reputation enhanced by a series of woodcuts of the carnage wreaked on London by the Blitz, was in demand by
London publishers. He also lectured at Ravensbourne College of Art in
Bromley for decades, alongside Peter (Fleischmann) Midgley, his fellow
alumnus. While his first wife Edith served him with divorce papers
during his internment and then moved to America with his son Florian,
he married Lesley McDonald in 1946, and together they established
their own influential imprint, Acorn Press.

Hermann Fechenbach contributed to the canon of Hutchinson literature, too. Although he never quite received the recognition enjoyed by
many of his peers, he produced *Genesis: The First Book of Moses*, replete
with 137 of his own prints, and *The Last Jews of Mergentheim*, part auto-
biography, part family history. Shortly before his death, his woodcuts
were exhibited in London, and *The Guardian* reviewer declared them "a
striking reminder of a forgotten talent."

Heinrich Fraenkel's résumé included authoritative biographies on Himmler, Hess, Hitler, and Göring (some co-authored with Roger Manvell), a study of German cinema, more works on the Nazi influence on his homeland, and a couple of highly acclaimed books on chess. The game he'd first mastered as a teen internee at Knockaloe in World War I remained a passion thereafter, and he wrote a popular, well-regarded chess column for *The New Statesman* magazine under the pseudonym "Assiac," the backwards spelling of Caissa, goddess of chess.

Decades later, it was not unusual for two ex-Hutchinson men to meet on a London street and to greet each other with phrases from Kurt Schwitters's discordant sound poem, *Ursonate*, which, of course, must have sounded like gobbledygook to anybody eavesdropping. Some characters, like Fred Uhlman and Paul Hamann, worked together in the Free German League of Culture and, for a time, denizens of the Artists' Café also used to meet on a regular basis at either the Maison Bertaux patisserie in Soho or at Hamann's studio in St. John's Wood.

After his death in 1973, the National Portrait Gallery purchased four of Hamann's life masks for its collection, a testimony to his contribution to British art. Ernst Müller-Blensdorf, another of the sculpting fraternity, became a teacher in Somerset and continued to produce highly regarded wood pieces, many touching on religious themes. Dr. Julius (Ulli) Hirsch emigrated to America, became director of business administration at the New School for Social Research in New York and adviser to the US government.

Fred Uhlman was released in December 1940 and arrived back to Hampstead as the clock was reaching midnight on New Year's Eve. Next day, he traveled to Essex to reunite with his wife Diana and to see his daughter Caroline for the first time. Just after the war ended, he published *Captivity*, a selection of his drawings produced during internment, including his signature haunting image of a girl holding a balloon. He exhibited his work widely over the ensuing decades without ever, he felt, turning into the great artist he had hoped to become.

In 1960, Uhlman published a memoir titled *The Making of an Englishman*, and, after a detached retina prematurely ended his artistic career, he wrote *Reunion*. A critically acclaimed novella about the friend-ship of two teenage boys, one the son of a Jewish doctor, the other of an aristocratic bent, it is set in 1930s Stuttgart amid the rise of Nazism. Made into a movie in 1986 with a screenplay by Harold Pinter, the book remains in print today, living up to Arthur Koestler's description of it as "a minor masterpiece." Although his art still sells, more people know him from the book perhaps than anything else.

"Why then do I want to tell the story of my internment, if it was such a non-event in the middle of a most horrible war?" asked Uhlman of his time at Hutchinson. "My answer is that, however small, it is part of the English history of the war, that for me and almost all of my friends it was not a trivial affair but a traumatic experience. The fact that millions suffered far more is no more relevant than to tell a man who lost one hand that others lost both arms and legs."

Of all the luminaries who spent time in the square, Schwitters remained the celebrity with the brightest wattage, once namedropped in a *Monty Python's Flying Circus* sketch about Picasso and other artistic giants participating in a cycling race, an absurdist accolade that would surely have appealed to him. Equally, he might have enjoyed the fact that when you search him out online these days, it is possible to buy, aside from books about him, a shopping bag containing one of his prints, a website selling miniature figurines of him, and a stamp issued by the German Post Office in his honor on the centenary of his birth. The very ephemera from which he might have made great art.

The way in which Schwitters's reputation has endured to this day is ironic considering how much of his life after Hutchinson was a perpetual struggle. Having moved to London upon release in November 1941, he had a one-man show that sold one piece, then learned his wife Helma had died of cancer back home, and the house where he had constructed the original *Merzbau* at Waldhausenstrasse 5 had been demolished by Allied bombs. In dire penury most of the time, he moved to the Lake District with his new companion, Edith Thomas, where, despite constant financial woes, he continued to produce.

In classic Schwitters style, he knocked great fun out of finishing third in a local painting competition, and with nobody around idyllic Ambleside interested in his more avant-garde stuff, eked out a living doing more commercial rural scenes. After years of toil, his fortunes finally improved when the Museum of Modern Art in New York awarded him a fellowship in 1947, the money affording him the chance to start another *Merzbau* in a hayloft. Three months into the project he contracted bronchitis and then developed pneumonia. Two days after his death, at age sixty, a letter arrived confirming he'd been accepted as a British citizen.

"He is the only major twentieth-century artist to have died in Britain," wrote art critic Waldemar Januszczak, "and nobody even knew he was here."

By the time Klaus Hinrichsen was released in June 1941, Hutchinson's heyday of the Barbed Wire University, the Artists' Café, and the classical concerts on the lawn was largely at an end due to the departure of so many luminaries. The camp continued to host a dwindling number of internees thereafter, and even POWs briefly toward the very end of the war. Then, the barbed wire was removed and the houses returned to the landladies. Some of the buildings remain bed-and-breakfasts to this day, and the only clue to their place in history are ornamental tiles discreetly placed around the square by Isle of Man art students commemorating some of the greats who once called this place home.

When he returned to London, Hinrichsen volunteered to serve in the Home Guard and married Gretel. At war's end, he visited Germany to discover his parents and brother had somehow survived the conflict; nevertheless, he chose to live the rest of his life in England. He carved out a successful career in the pharmaceutical industry. The couple opened a beloved toy shop on the Archway Road, and worked tirelessly for liberal causes. In his spare time, Hinrichsen deployed his art historian background to excellent effect, becoming the unofficial chronicler and champion of all things Hutchinson. Keeper of the flame. Custodian of the narrative.

In the 1990s, James Taylor, then a researcher at the Imperial War Museum in London, was browsing a bookstore on Charing Cross Road when he came across a typescript, bound together between cardboard, purporting to be an account of life at "P Camp"—the Home Office designation for Hutchinson. The museum purchased the manuscript, which gave a comprehensive subject-by-subject breakdown of life around the square, covering everything from the library to the various schools in great detail. It was signed by a P. Beckert, but once Hinrichsen ran his eyes across it he detected the handiwork of the inimitable and dubious Ludwig Warschauer.

In depicting life in the camp, the author went to great lengths in his thirty-nine pages to laud the Technical School and the man behind it, and to praise Commander Daniel and the authorities at every turn. Hinrichsen was so incensed by this skewed portrayal that he put together a lengthy rebuttal, a paragraph-by-paragraph takedown, under the heading "Scholars Beware." To sift through the alleged Warschauer pamphlet and Hinrichsen's ruthless parsing of it, there's an obvious conclusion to be drawn. The first work was written by a man trying to effect his own release, because, even in 1942, long after almost all of the men who'd entered in 1940 were gone, the head of the Technical School remained in custody. With good reason.

"Warschauer is known to be a man of generally bad character, a persistent and unscrupulous liar, and to have a limitless capacity for intrigue," wrote Brigadier Sir David Petrie, explaining why in 1942 he had recommended that the German be detained at Brixton Prison rather than any internment camp. "In particular we were anxious that the work of intelligence officers in London or Isle of Man internment camps should not be stultified by his denunciation of innocent internees and that he should be interned in a place where he would have no scope for such activities."

At the end of the war, Warschauer was deported back to Germany where, some of his fellow internees heard, he again carved out a prosperous career for himself. Whether or not that was true, Hinrichsen was not going to allow him to distort the record of what happened in the camp and how life was lived there. Not when he had dedicated himself to telling that story every chance he could. Hinrichsen gave lectures, he did interviews, and he wrote. Extensively. All in the service of the great men he lived with whom he felt should be better remembered by history.

None more so than his good friend Schwitters.

Following one appearance on BBC radio discussing life with Schwitters on the Isle of Man, Hinrichsen was contacted by a landscape architect from Scotland. The man's father had bequeathed him an album of paintings and sketches that the internees of Hutchinson Camp had created and gifted to him in 1941. The caller was Peter Daniel, son of the commander who had always treasured this book that was signed by so many of the artistic luminaries, all those years ago. The artwork contained in it, the art produced in internment, provided more evidence of how fecund life had somehow been behind that barbed wire.

"It is an ironic footnote to those days when we were His Majesty's most loyal enemy aliens," wrote Hinrichsen, "that it should be our jailer who has kept the record intact."

Select Bibliography

Books

Ash, Mitchell G., and Alfons Sollner. *Forced Migration and Scientific Change*. Cambridge, UK: Cambridge University Press, 1996.

Balfour, Michael (ed.). *Theatre and War 1933– 1945: Performance in Extremis*. New York: Berghahn Books, 2001.

Brinson, Charmian, Anna Muller-Harlin, and Julia Winckler. *His Majesty's Loyal Internee: Fred Uhlman in Captivity*. London: Valentine Mitchell, 2009.

Cesarani, David, and Tony Kushner (eds.). *The Internment of Aliens in Twentieth Century Britain*. London: Frank Cass and Company, Ltd., 1993.

Chappell, Connery. *Island of Barbed Wire: Internment on the Isle of Man in World War Two*. London: Robert Hale, 2005.

Cooper, R. M. (ed.). *Refugee Scholars: Conversations with Tess Simpson*. Leeds, England: Moorland Books, 1992.

Crawford, Sally, Katharina Ulmschneider, and Jas Elsner. *Ark of Civilization: Refugee Scholars and Oxford University 1930–1945*. Oxford: Oxford University Press, 2017.

Cresswell, Yvonne (ed.). *Living with the Wire*. Isle of Man: Manx National Heritage, 1994.

Dove, Richard (ed.). *Totally Un-English? Britain's Internment of "Enemy Aliens" in Two World Wars*. Amsterdam: Rodopi, 1994.

Fraenkel, Heinrich. *Help Us Germans to Beat the Nazis!* London: Victory Books, 1941.

Franklin, Alan. *Involuntary Guests*. Isle of Man: Lily Publications, 2017.

Gill, Irene. *Oma, Mu and Me*. Oxford: Yarnells Books, 2009.

Gillman, Peter, and Leni Gillman. *Collar the Lot!* London: Quartet Books, 1980.

Hemming, Henry. *The Ingenious Mr. Pyke: Inventor, Fugitive, Spy*. New York: Public Affairs, 2015.

Hill, Roland. *A Time Out of Joint*. London: Radcliffe Press, 2007.

Kochan, Miriam. *Britain's Internees in the Second World War*. London: Macmillan Press, 1983.

Kurlander, Eric. *Hitler's Monsters: A Supernatural History of the Third Reich*. New Haven, CT: Yale University Press, 2017.

Lafitte, Francois. *The Internment of Aliens*. London: Penguin Books, 1940.

London, Louise. *Whitehall and the Jews, 1933– 1948*. Cambridge: Cambridge University Press, 2000.

Motherwell, Robert (ed.). *The Dada Painters and Poets*. Cambridge: Belknap, 1981.

Nagorski, Tom. *Miracles on the Water.* New York: Hyperion, 2006.

Nyburg, Anna. *From Leipzig to London: The Life and Work of the Émigré Artist Hellmuth Weissenborn.* New Castle, DE: Oak Knoll Press, 2012.

Pistol, Rachel. *Internment during the Second World War: A Comparative Study of Great Britain and the USA.* London: Bloomsbury Academic, 2017.

Presler, Gerd, and Erik Riedel. *Ludwig Meidner: Catalogue Raisonne of His Sketchbooks.* Munich, Germany: Prestel, 2013.

Snowman, Daniel. *The Hitler Émigrés: The Cultural Impact on Britain of Refugees from Nazism.* London: Chatto & Windus, 2002.

Stent, Gunther S. *Nazis, Women and Molecular Biology: Memoirs of a Lucky Self-Hater.* Kensington: Briones Books, 1998.

Stent, Ronald. *A Bespattered Page? The Internment of His Majesty's "Most Loyal Enemy Aliens."* London: Andre Deutsch, 1980.

Trauman Steinitz, Kate. *Kurt Schwitters: A Portrait from Life.* Berkeley: University of California Press, 1968.

Uhlman, Fred. *The Making of an Englishman.* London: Victor Gollancz, 1960.

Zühlsdorff, Volkmar. *Hitler's Exiles: The German Cultural Resistance in America and Europe.* London: Continuum, 2004.

NEWSPAPERS

Association of Jewish Refugees Journal
The Camp newspaper (https://archive.org/details/thecampmf1465)
The Guardian
Isle of Man Times
The Observer
Ramsey Courier
Reynold's News

ARCHIVES

Imperial War Museum Oral History Collection

Friedenthal, Richard (Catalog Number 3963)
Hallgarten, Fritz (Catalog Number 3967)
Hinrichsen, Klaus (Catalog Number 3789)
Midgley, Peter (Catalog Number 3941)
Munster, Rudolph (Catalog Number 3899)
Stent, Ronald (Catalog Number 22209)
Weissenborn, Hellmuth (Catalog Number 3771)

Family Sources

Furth, Hans (video interview provided by the Furth family)
Mirecki, Adolf (additional details provided by his son Daniel)

National Archives (London) Files
HO 214/60 Leo Freund / Michael Corvin
KV 2/1142 Ludwig Max WARSCHAUER

Manx National Heritage Library, Douglas, Isle of Man
MS 08166. Second World War Internment Camps: Nazi intelligence network in an Isle of Man camp. Newspaper cuttings and letters on this topic explored by Mr. Rock of Liverpool. 1970s FONDS Letters and newspaper cuttings.

MS 09299. Sketch of garden plan; blank entry form for Isle of Man Internment Camp, c.1940s; FONDS sketch; entry form, 2 papers, pencil sketch on brown paper of a garden plan labeled in German; empty "entry form" for Isle of Man Internment Camp. Found behind paneling at 37 Hutchinson Square.

MS 10739. Account of internment at P Camp, Hutchinson Square.

MS 11443. Memoirs of Alfred (Freddy) C. Godshaw, onetime internee at Hutchinson Camp, together with 2006 e-mail correspondence with Alan Franklin and a copy of his submission on the WW2 People's War website (https://www.bbc.co.uk/history/ww2peopleswar/user/91/u1115291.shtml).

MS 11622. Drawing of Hutchinson Square with accompanying pages from an exercise book.

MS 11626. Undated memoirs of Professor Paul Jacobsthal

MS 11643. Papers of Harry Paul Cemach, onetime internee in Hutchinson Camp, Douglas, during 1940.

MS 11895. Home Office internment general file (subseries "communications"), concerning the loss of money from registered mail addressed to internees, and including details of appeals from men interned on the Isle of Man.

MS 12198. "A Hutchinson Camp March" ("Song of the Internees"), with words and music by Edward E. Verdiers.

MS 12841. Open letter from the Commandant, Isle of Man Internment Camps, addressed "To the Internees of the Isle of Man," June 1, 1940.

House of Commons Debates
Hansard: July 10, 1940, vol. 362, 1208–306; November 7, 1940, vol. 365, 1504–31; November 20, 1940, vol. 365, 1988–93; W. House of Lords Debate, October 24, 1939, Hansard, vol. 114, 1487.

INDEX

About the Author

Dave Hannigan is a professor of history at Suffolk County Community College on Long Island and a weekly columnist with the *Irish Times* in Dublin. Author of several nonfiction books, he's a native of Cork and currently resides in East Setauket, New York, with his sons Abe, Charlie, and Finn.